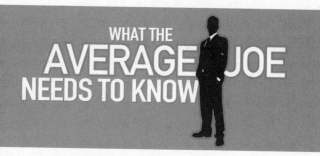

WHAT THE
AVERAGE JOE
NEEDS TO KNOW

THE NINE
RULES OF
CREDIT

Praise for "The Nine Rules of Credit"

Going through a bankruptcy is stressful but trying to rebuild your credit after is even worse. After working with Richard Moxley and following the Nine Rules of Credit, I no longer have any restrictions or hassles when it comes to applying for financing. I am also once again eligible for the best discounted rates which will save me thousands of dollars, in the years to come!

– Dr Andrew

As a Financial Advisor I am constantly asked for ways to help my clients with their debt issues and how to save money. I will continue to recommend your simple and easy to use guide on how to start, improve, maintain and protect ones credit to clients, friends, family, and even other professional's in the financial industry.

– David Williams CFP

Becoming a Canadian Citizen doesn't automatically give you the basic financial know how to succeed in a new country, especially when it comes to credit. That is why I was so happy to meet Richard and attend one of his credit seminars. Armed with the knowledge of the Nine Rules of Credit and industry secrets I no longer fear working with the banks or wonder about how to protect my credit.

– Elisa Mikan

As first time home-buyers, we knew the end goal but were unsure on how to get there. After being referred to Richard and learning the Nine Rules of Credit, we now have a roadmap on exactly what we have to do to achieve our goals step by step. Who knew having great credit was more than just paying your bills on time.

– Heather and Scott Ransome

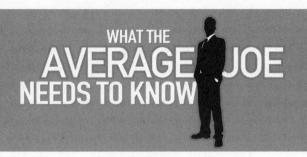

WHAT THE
AVERAGE JOE
NEEDS TO KNOW

THE NINE
RULES OF
CREDIT

How to Start, Rebuild, and
Always Maintain Great Credit

Richard Moxley

Note: This book has been published in Canada.
Though the content is useful for any market, please note
that all amounts are in Canadian dollars.

For information about permission to reproduce sections of this
book, email Richard Moxley at:

richard@theaveragejoebook.com

Cataloguing data available from Library and Archives Canada

Printed in Canada

This book is dedicated to my best friend, my wife and of course the "monsters" that I love Ben, Ellie, Addisyn and any other future children. Thank you to the rest of my family for their support and ideas. To everyone else that has influenced my life and the creation of this book; any success I have is because of you.

What I mean by the "Average Joe"

Some people have questioned me on why I named the book "What the Average Joe Needs to Know". Are you just average? Of course not! You are one of a kind, and great at whatever you do whether it is being a mom, an Astronaut, a business owner, a student or a good friend. However, when it comes to different subjects, especially finances, many of us are just "Average". My vision for the Average Joe book series is to take different financial topics and educate the average Canadian on what you NEED to know to save money. That way you can focus your time and energy on what you love and enjoy your life to the fullest!

Knowledge is the new currency. It enriches your own life and helps everyone else, when you share it! So… PASS IT ON!!

Preface

If you live in North America, it is safe to assume that you are carrying at least one form of debt, be it a credit card, a school or car loan, or a mortgage. Even if you don't have any debt, and you live on this continent, you are forced to play the credit game! Yep, that's right, a real-life game with rules to follow, strategies for success, penalties for failure, and even personal rankings known as your credit score. How well you play this game will not only determine your interest rates, but also whether you get approved for a property of your own, a place to rent, a job promotion, or even a parking spot. If you don't know all of the Nine Rules of Credit, no worries – you're the "average Joe", and this book is for you!

Think you have good credit? You may be paying your bills on time, but what about the other eight rules? If promptness is the only rule you know, what's the likelihood of you wrecking your credit, unknowingly? I am not a gambling man, but even I can see that the odds are not good. Is this a chance you're willing to take, with so much riding on your credit? You need to learn all the rules in order to play this game well.

For the average Joe, applying for any type of financing, including credit, can be a scary and complicated process. Let me assure you that I've done everything possible to make this book a completely different experience for you. I think the average Joe learns best through stories, and so, I've tried to demonstrate all my main points with real-life stories based on my clients' experiences (changing the names in each case to protect my clients' privacy). I have also added some personal stories of my own.

As a licensed mortgage agent, I have come to know how bankers are trained to think about credit, because I've been dealing with them on a daily basis since 2006. I have spoken with the credit reporting agencies on numerous occasions (the companies that rank you on your gameplay), and have met and had lunch with the underwriters who review your loan applications. I have also witnessed, first hand, thousands of different scenarios that can happen to your credit score, depending on whether you follow the Nine Rules of Credit or not. It doesn't matter if you are just starting out, rebuilding your credit or just trying to maintain the credit you already have. I promise to teach you the inside credit secrets and all the helpful tips I've learned along the way.

"Knowledge is power," as the saying goes. The truths you can learn from this book will not only allow you to always be approved, based on your credit, but will also save you hundreds of thousands of dollars over your lifetime. Derek Bok, an American educator said it best with this quote, "If you think education is expensive, try ignorance." That's why I know this book will be a great source of help to you. With the information inside these pages, you will always be able to play to win.

Table of Contents

Chapter 1

Introduction – My Passion for Credit

So there I was sitting on an overturned bucket in the backyard of some friends in a village just outside of Salta, Argentina when Hermano Gomez asked me if I thought he should apply for a credit card. Are you kidding me? Here? This family? They lived in what would be considered, by North American standards, to be a shack, with only two rooms with dirt floors, and no indoor plumbing. Hermano Gomez had three children and a wife, all crammed into this tiny, tin-roofed home. The taxi my companion and I took to get to this family's house was, I'm sure, one of the first cars ever off the assembly line. The majority of the houses in the area didn't have phones or microwaves, and owning a personal computer was reserved for the very wealthy. "So why a credit card?" I asked. "To buy a new television, of course," the family responded.

One thing South Americans share with North Americans is a passion for TV. But in Latino countries, it is used primarily for watching soccer. Although it is common to see a house without a real door and glassless windows, the roof often sports a satellite dish so that they can follow their favorite soccer team and watch the occasional Novella (Spanish soap opera).

It was 2004 and I had been in rural South America for over a year. I was becoming accustomed to the carefree lifestyle that the people there enjoyed so much. Few owned watches; no one had cell phones; there was no such thing as rush-hour traffic, and nobody owed any debt, which made everyone there so much more relaxed. There were no such things as mortgages, loans, or credit cards. That is why I was so shocked when Hermano Gomez asked me for advice on credit. As so many of us do, I repeated to him what my parents told me: Credit cards are like the devil: fun at first, but they have a tendency to burn you in the end. Maybe I didn't use those exact words, but I had no clue about credit, except that it could be dangerous. It always seemed to be such a huge burden for anyone that became dependent upon it. My advice was simply to stay away from credit, because like most people, I knew little about it.

When I returned home to Canada in the middle of 2005, I was quickly immersed back into the "real world," where the "buy-now, pay-later" mentality was just the usual way of life. Not long after my return to Canada, I decided to become a mortgage broker. Less than two years earlier I had advised the wonderful family in Argentina to avoid credit cards and debt all together, and now I was doing a 180-degree turn by helping fellow Canadians get into huge amounts of debt. However, I believe that mortgages are a different kind of debt; they are a necessary evil in North America. Most of the top financial gurus call this type of financing good debt, as opposed to bad debt, which is debt unsecured to a house, a car or another asset. I personally don't label anything that takes money out of my pocket as a "good" thing, no matter what it may be attached to. The only assets I want to have in my portfolio are ones that continue to put money into my pocket on a regular basis. Of course, my wife and my kids are the only exceptions to this rule!

Once I started working at a national mortgage brokerage, I learned a lot about finances and even more about credit.

Just like most new mortgage agents, it was up to me to find my own clients. I was starting all over again in a brand new industry. Because I am fluent in Spanish, having spent two years in Argentina as a missionary for the Latter-Day Saints church(LDS), I came up with what I thought was a great idea. I would help Spanish-speaking families with their mortgage financing. I had no problem finding families who wanted to buy their own homes instead of renting them. I was ecstatic about all the success I was having, but then I kept running into one very big problem. Many of my clients had little or no established Canadian credit. Even though my niche clients were employed and had managed to save up their down payment, very few banks and mortgage lenders would provide their mortgage financing without them having established credit. It is true that there are programs called "New to Canada" that allow you to use alternative forms of credit, but this is aimed at families who have been in Canada for less than three years.

I continued to work with families who qualified as "New to Canada," but, because I needed more business to survive, I also began working with first-time homebuyers. As a twenty-three year old myself, I figured that this was the typical age of other young persons who wished to buy their first property. I found many young Canadians interested in purchasing their first home; yet, I ran into the same problem as with my new-to-Canada clients. Although these young people were gainfully employed, and had saved or been gifted money for the down payment, their credit history was limited. Once again, many of the banks and mortgage lenders would not accept people from this category for mortgage financing.

You may think that people from the younger age group or those new-to-Canada were the only categories that had problems with credit, and that I would have more success working with those with more life experience. Sadly, I learned that this was not always the case. A person's age seemed to have little bearing on how established their credit was. This was driving me nuts; almost everyone I received an application from was either denied a mortgage, because they had no credit history, or they had been forced into higher interest rates due to having bad credit. It became apparent to me that the average Canadian had no clue how to achieve, maintain, or improve their credit. It made no difference whether they were new-to-Canada, first-time homebuyers, or just the average Joe.

I started to spend more time with my clients, reviewing their credit history with them. I learned that very few of them had ever seen their own credit report, and no one seemed to know how to improve a poor one. Credit reports are copies of all your credit account information that is received by both Equifax and TransUnion. Equifax and TransUnion are the two major credit reporting agencies in Canada and in the world. Their job is to take all the individual credit accounts that you have and then rank you based on a scoring system. Your credit score is also known as a Beacon score, Empirical score, Fair Isaac (or FICO) score, which are all different names that basically refer to the same thing. They are names which individual companies use to describe how well you are doing at following the Nine Rules of Credit.

Growing up, I was never taught the rules of credit, and any time the subject of credit was brought up, it was usually during a heated debate between my parents that I didn't stick around to hear! Luckily, my father did give me one piece of solid financial advice: Pay your bills on time! Sound familiar? The problem was that neither my father, nor any of the education I received, ever taught me about the other eight rules of credit. It's funny how parents can give you such great advice, and then forget to tell you how to go about achieving it. An even worse case is when your parents or teachers give you outdated or wrong information that they still swear by. I can just imagine what my parents learned about credit in the "good old days."

After years of reading and reviewing hundreds of credit reports, I started to realize that TransUnion, Equifax, and even the banks did not think like the rest of us. No wonder going into the bank and applying for credit is such a scary thing for most people to do. The average Joe has no clue why he is being denied credit, nor where to begin to find answers. Even those who think they have great credit need to know what shows up on their credit report. If you don't know how you got there, or what makes your score go down, you're putting yourself and your financial future at a huge risk. It was at this time that I had my "Ah ha" moment and decided to teach as many people as possible the rules to having great credit.

Life gets crazy, and until we have a problem with credit we assume that we know these rules already. Most of us are unaware that if we follow some very simple steps, the game of credit would be so much easier to play. How much time would you spend in the penalty box if you were playing hockey, but didn't know the rules? The answer is: too much! While it is true that you can always repair your credit over time, I'm not talking about a five-minute penalty for a major rule violation. I'm talking about six or seven years! No wonder people have a bad taste in their mouth when it comes to credit. Have no fear, because when you are armed with insider knowledge, you can either completely avoid the problem or improve your credit at an expedited rate. In the following chapters, I will explain the Nine Rules of Credit in full detail, along with some other important credit and money-saving tips.

Let's get started

The most popular question I am asked at my credit seminars is, "How do I get started?"

If you don't already have a recent copy of both your TransUnion and Equifax credit reports, now would be a great time to get them.

Here is how you can do that:

For your TransUnion Report, go to www.transunion.ca. It will cost you $14.95 for your credit report, and $7.95 for your credit score, for a total of $22.90.

Visit www.equifax.ca to get the Equifax copy of your credit report. They give you two options. You can order your report with or without the score on it. It will cost you $24.95 with the score, or $19.95 without.

I am also frequently asked if it's worth paying the extra money in order to get the score. For the purpose of this book, on learning and understanding where you are in the credit game, I suggest you pay the extra money to know your score. I will go through why your credit score is so important in the next chapter.

Money-saving tip

Get your report for free

Please be aware that you can obtain a free copy of your credit report by mailing a request into each agency. Also, TransUnion has a handful of local stores where you can pick up your report in person. To find a list of locations, go to my web site under lists and forms. By law, each credit-reporting agency must provide you with one free report, when requested, every 12 months. However, these free copies contain the report only; they don't show your actual credit score. You can go to the credit reporting agencies' respective web sites to find an application form, and directions on how to submit your request to each agency. You can also go to my web site at www. TheAverageJoeBook.com and under lists and tools you will find direct links to everything you will need.

Next step

Once you have a copy of both credit reports, go through them in detail to make sure everything is correct and up-to-date. Note any mistakes; I'm sure there will be some, and I'll go through the process on how to get it sorted out further on in the book.

Chapter 1 – Avergae Joe Action Steps

1. Go to www.TransUnion.ca and request your credit report with your credit score. Go to www.Equifax.ca and request your credit report and your credit score.

2. If you don't have your own credit card with which to order online, go to my website at: www.The AverageJoeBook.com to find locations where you can obtain your credit report in person.

Chapter 2

The Credit Score Basics

When you purchase that nice, new 70-inch flat-screen TV with your credit card, all your information is sent, electronically, to the credit reporting agencies. Every time you make, delay, or miss a payment, on any type of account, that information is also recorded. Both TransUnion and Equifax, the two major reporting agencies, will use that data to determine if you are a credit risk or not. Put in simple terms, you will be ranked depending on how much you will cost a bank or lender. One way they do this is by providing each adult Canadian with a credit score. It may be helpful if you imagine your credit score as if it were your Grade Point Average (GPA) from your high school or post-secondary institution. Then consider your individual credit accounts, such as credit cards, lines of credit, and loans, as your individual courses.

Your credit GPA (credit score), which is the sum of all your accounts, helps potential lenders quickly analyze how you are doing in the credit game. Unlike a GPA, your credit score will be different with each credit-reporting agency, as each company has a different way of grading that same account information. Don't be alarmed by these small variations; just keep in mind that Equifax and TransUnion have slightly different algorithms. An algorithm is just a fancy word for a computer process that categorizes your information into a format that the average Joe can understand. Other than the irregularities in each company's algorithms, your score from either company may be different because not every bank or lender reports to both credit agencies. It costs banks and lenders time and money to submit information to both reporting agencies, so some just report to either one or the other. That is why you could have an account show up on one report and not on the other and why it's important for Canadians to request and review both your Equifax and TransUnion credit reports. To reiterate, why it is so important to review both credit reports, I will share an experience I had with two of my clients.

Malik and Marie had just moved to Calgary from Quebec, and after getting settled, they went looking to purchase a property. I had their application set up and ready to go. It looked like they would qualify for the home they wanted to purchase. When I review a client's mortgage application with them, I always ask them if they have ever claimed bankruptcy. When these two told me no, I quickly went on to the next question, not thinking anything of it because nothing bad showed up on their Equifax Report. Everything else on the application looked good, but to my surprise, it came back declined. I called the underwriter right away and asked her what was going on. She informed me that she had also looked at their TransUnion Report, and found that my clients had been discharged from a bankruptcy a couple of years earlier. I went back to the clients to see if that had actually happened, and their response was, "Oh, that bankruptcy. We finished paying that, like, three years ago." I hope you learn a couple of things from this story. First of all, because different accounts will show up with different agencies, you need to check both your credit reports in order to get the whole picture. And of course, don't lie on credit applications, especially on ones you send to me!

In their defense, I don't think Malik and Marie meant to lie. I'm sure they just assumed that once they had been discharged their bankruptcy wouldn't show up on their report anymore, so why would it matter? Being discharged from a bankruptcy means your debt has been repaid and you have no more financial responsibilities to your previous creditors. However, this doesn't stop it from showing up on your credit, and therefore, you will need to disclose this information when applying for financing.

If I had been told about their discharged bankruptcy before submitting the application to the bank, I could have either provided a good reason as to why it happened in the first place, or saved time by working with a lender who would have been okay with a previous bankruptcy.

Credit scores are like a first impression

The commonly used saying, "You never get a second chance to make a first impression" is crucial to remember when looking at the importance of your credit score. As banks and lenders review thousands of applications a day, without a high credit score, yours may be put at the bottom of the pile or turned down without someone even going through it. When you hear a student has a 4.0 GPA in school, it gives you the sense that they are smart. With your "credit GPA" or credit score, the higher the score, the better your first impression to the banks will be.

On both your Equifax and TransUnion reports, you will have a score between 300 and 900. I'm sure you have seen many different pictures of ranking scales online, but most scales are misleading. The reason these scales are deceptive is because most come from the US, which differs from ours in Canada, and because each type of financing has different guidelines. Mortgage financing is one of the hardest types of credit to qualify for. Therefore, if your credit is considered amazing in the mortgage category, then you shouldn't have any issues in any of the others.

A credit score ranking system intended for mortgage financing, would look like this:

Poor	Fair	Good	Excellent	Amazing
300-575	576-629	630-679	680-750	751-900

In addition to a bad first impression, your credit score will determine the interest rate or fees that you will be charged. For example, if when you go to apply for a car loan, and you have amazing credit or a score between 751 to 900, then you will get the best, discounted rate. You also won't pay any fees other than the basic "set-up fees" or other expenses that they charge everyone. If you are in the poor or fair credit category, then, the lenders will apply higher interest rates. The lower your credit score the more it will cost you.

Banks and lenders are a business; they don't lend money to be nice they do it to make profits. A credit score gives them the ability to categorize their potential profitability and charge you accordingly. To summarize, having a high credit score gives you a great first impression and highly influences your cost to borrow.

Chapter 2 – Average Joe Action Step

1. Review and familiarize yourself with each report. Then circle any errors you may find.

Chapter 3

It Always Pays to Have Good Credit

Good credit will save you hundreds of thousands of dollars, and maybe even millions of dollars, over your lifetime!

I know you may be thinking that the interest rate you qualify for is only 1% or 2% higher with bad credit than for good credit, so is the score really that important? You may even be able to afford the higher payments required with a lower score. So what is the big deal?

It is, in fact, a very big deal. Have you ever been punched in the shoulder? Maybe a friend or older sibling? Yes I speak from experience! The first time it may hurt a bit, but you usually suck it up so you can convince yourself and others it was no big deal. However, when your older sisters take turns hitting the same spot over and over again (Obviously I have some unresolved childhood issues) those little punches start to add up. Think of the banks as your older sisters taking swings at you because your credit is bad. The high interest payments really start to hurt.

Here are some examples on just how much great credit can save you over a lifetime.

Mortgages

The following chart outlines your savings based on which category of credit you are in.

Based on a $300,000 5-year fixed mortgage, with monthly payments over a 25-year amortization (life of the mortgage)					
			Savings		
Credit Type	Rate	Payment	Monthly	Over 5 years	Over 25 years
Excellent/ Amazing credit (680+)	3.09%	$1,433.63	$510.83	$30,649.80	$153,249.00
Good Credit (630-679)	3.29%	$1,464.75	$479.71	$28,782.60	$143,913.00
Fair Credit (576-629)	4.64%	$1,683.85	$260.61	$15,636.60	$78,183.00
Poor Credit (300-575)	6.14%	$1,944.46	N/A	N/A	N/A

If you are the average Joe, having over $150,000 in your back pocket should be incentive enough to always have amazing credit; but hold on, we are just getting started.

With bad credit, not only are you paying higher interest rates, you can also expect to be charged upfront lending fees. Think of these fees as risk insurance for the lender. The more risky you are, the higher the fee. Depending on how bad your credit is, as well as other qualifying factors, your fees will generally be within one to ten percent of the mortgage amount. Whether you keep the mortgage for a year or just a month, you will still pay the same upfront fee.

For example, let's say you had a 550 Beacon score (credit score). Your starting fees would be 3% of the entire mortgage amount. On a $300,000 mortgage amount, you are not only paying over $500 a month, but $9,000 in upfront fees. Once again, that money is better in your pocket than in someone else's.

Trust me when I say that the numbers in the previous chart are very conservative for a rate and fee increase with someone who has bad credit. Here's another example to illustrate a more average cost of bad credit.

Take the Robinson family; they have two mortgages totalling $320,000 on a house that is worth approximately $450,000. They are making monthly payments of $3,250 when they could be paying only $1,529.20 per month, if their credit was good. They are basically throwing away $1,720.80 per month because of not following the Nine Rules of Credit. That means they are paying a total of $103,248 extra over a five-year period, due to higher interest rates. If they didn't improve their credit over that five years, and continued that trend for the life of the mortgage, it would cost them $516,240. This cost is above and beyond the original house price and typical mortgage interest and charges that come along with home ownership.

I am so glad that I graduated knowing how to dissect a frog and how to find the square root of 600, but where was the class on credit? I am not saying that science and math aren't important, but just ask the Robinson's which information would have been more practical.

Money-saving tip

Want to have a guaranteed rate of return on your investment? How about making additional payments to your mortgage or car loans? A small lump sum like $500 a year in extra payments can bring you double-digit savings on interest; $500 a year is only $1.36 a day. You can also save money over the long term by switching your loan payments to bi-weekly or even weekly payments instead of the traditional monthly payments. This forces you to make two to four extra payments a year, which all goes to paying down your debt faster and saves you money. For prepayment mortgage and loan calculators to estimate how much you can save, go to www. TheAverageJoeBook.com, click on the tools and list tab, and click on calculators.

Car loans, personal loans, lines of credit, and even credit cards all work the same way as mortgages. Being charged a higher interest rate may not seem like much on a monthly basis, but over the years it adds up.

Credit can even affect your employment

The list of cons to not having good credit is endless, but not knowing the Nine Rules of Credit can even prevent you from getting certain jobs or promotions. Accountant certifications and trustees are examples of two professions where your title can be delayed or taken away based partially on your credit history. Whether it's in a financial institution or any other cash or account handling position, it is common to have a credit check done before you qualify for the job. Employers who perform these credit checks feel that you're less trustworthy if you have bad credit due to incorrect handling of your own finances. Even though there may be extenuating circumstances, any attempt to explain your own poor credit rating may sound like an excuse rather than a legitimate reason.

Beth, one of my clients, is an excellent example of how bad credit limited her earning power. Beth was an accountant and wanted to get a higher certification in the same field, but was not able to because of her credit history. Just because she didn't know some of the simple rules of credit, she missed out on her certification and lost an opportunity for a sizable pay increase. In Beth's case, she would have been eligible for a $40,000/year raise, if only she had better credit. That is a huge amount to lose year after year. During the two years that it will take for her to improve her credit in order to qualify for the promotion and the higher designation, she will lose $80,000.

Restrictive options in life

For those who haven't maintained good credit, there is something worse than it costing you more money, and that is less options. In 2008, we saw the banks become much more restrictive on lending practices because of the US subprime meltdown. This financial mess didn't only affect the United States mortgage industry, it put the US into a recession, and almost every other country felt the effects of it. The recession or downturn in the economy put banks and investors on edge, and now everyone has to have even better credit than they did before the crisis.

I'm sure if you stop and think about it, you could come up with a few examples of how your options would be limited with bad credit. I'm sure you have thought of setbacks like not being approved for a mortgage, a car loan, or even being able to get a place to rent. These are all true, but here are some additional things that you may not have thought of! Shopping online by credit card, setting up a cell phone account or a home security system, and even your utilities, such as electricity and heat, can be restricted due to a low credit score. Life without a credit card is more difficult when booking a flight, reserving tickets, leasing a car, renting a room, or even parking downtown.

As I've demonstrated, knowing how to achieve and always maintain good credit can save you hundreds, thousands, or even millions of dollars. Not having to be restricted or embarrassed in any way, because you've been declined for credit or that promotion you've been working so hard for is . . . PRICELESS!

Now it is time to learn exactly what it takes to have good credit. The following chapters will outline the Nine Rules of Credit that you and every other average Joe should know and review constantly.

Chapter 4

Rule 1: Pay Your Bills on Time

This is the common-sense rule that I thought I understood until I read my credit report. I then realized that I was not as diligent as I should have been. A late payment does hurt your score, but it lowers your score even more with each month it is late.

For example, if you forget to pay your minimum monthly payment, but pay it within a 30-day time frame, it will lower your score, but not near as much if it is not paid within a 60-day time frame. Once you are 90-days late or more, you're really hurting your account and this will continue until you get your account up-to-date. The more this happens with multiple accounts, or more regularly, the more it can destroy your credit.

What if you have a good excuse?

Very rarely do lending companies care about the sequence of events leading up to your delinquent or missed payment. When you signed the contract, you agreed to the conditions. Unfortunately for me, my wife feels the same way, which leaves me with very few acceptable excuses.

Nowadays, everything is electronic and computers don't have any sympathy! If you call in and speak with an employee, many times they have no power to change things already registered in the system. Even if it's a company error, you will still be hard-pressed to get things changed in a timely manner. Loans and lines of credit are the same, it all depends on the policy of each bank, so train yourself to pay early.

Tips on how to remember to pay on time

Once again, the first step is to know your due date. And no, not all payments are due at the beginning or the end of the month. The truth is that the due date varies with every card or loan that you have. If, for some reason, the due date is not displayed clearly on the statement, you can call in and a customer service representative will let you know when each payment is due. As well, don't assume that because you didn't get charged extra interest or some kind of penalty, that it didn't negatively affect your credit. Sometimes a good tearjerker story will convince the service rep to waive the fee or the extra interest, but that doesn't guarantee that it hasn't already been electronically reported on your credit history.

Next, come up with a way to simplify the process. Money is generally already automatically taken out of your account for loans, so ensure you have money in the account. With credit cards and lines of credit, remembering to pay on time can be a bit harder. Here is a trick that I use – one that I think will help the average Joe to be sure to never miss a payment again. Pay your typical regular minimum balance at the very beginning of the month. In order for this to work, you need to know what your minimum monthly payment is, and how it is calculated. Once again, this information can be found on your statement or you can call the customer service agent. For example, if you generally spend $1,000 dollars a month on your credit accounts and your minimum monthly payment is $30, and then make two payments a month. Make a $30 or $50 payment to cover the minimum payment and then make a payment five business days before your due date to pay the rest of the balance off, if you can. That way, if life gets busy toward the end of the month and you forget, you are guaranteed not to have a late payment show up on your credit report.

You can increase your success rate by automating the payment process. Your bank should have a way to allow you to make automatic payments online or through the branch. If you have all your bills paid automatically, and you have overdraft protection (talk to your banker about this option) on your bank account, you can eliminate late payments. The bills still get paid, even if you are on holidays or you have an emergency. However, under this system, if you change your bank account, you have to ensure that each creditor is made aware of the change.

If you don't want everything automatically paid, you can set a recurring email or electronic calendar alert to help you keep track of all your different payment obligations. If you are "old school," you can achieve the same results by marking the dates on your paper calendar. However, make sure you do it for the entire year at one time, so you don't forget a month.

I frequently get asked if paying your balance down to zero each month will improve your credit. As long as the minimum balance is paid each month, that is all the lending institutions require. Banks and credit card companies don't want you to pay back what you owe all at once, because the longer it takes, and the higher your balance is, the more money they make. Obviously, my suggestion would be to pay your balance in full each month to avoid paying high interest rates.

One strategy to help build your credit faster is to make multiple payments on your card each month. This won't increase your credit score, but it builds a positive relationship with your lender. Bank reps have also confirmed to me that the more payments you make each month, the more favourable it looks on their internal processes, especially with loan payments.

Which bills show up on your credit report:

It is also important to know what is on your credit report. Suppose you find yourself in a financial bind and you have to choose which bills you're going to pay first that month. You should pay the bills that will affect your credit the most. By no means am I suggesting that you shouldn't pay certain bills, but if there are times when extreme circumstances arise, such as an illness, death in the family, or loss of employment, you may have to make choices. During such times, when you can't pay all your bills, it's good to know that bills such as rent, heat, hydro, water, phone, cable, and taxes don't affect your credit score right away. However, if these bills go unpaid for a number of consecutive months, they will be sent to collections.

Once your bill is with a collection company, they will immediately register the judgment on your credit report. Collection companies specialize in finding and collecting outstanding debts and provide services on behalf of the banks and lenders. As soon as you pay bills that have been forwarded to a collection agency, they will show as paid, and your credit score will start improving again. If you don't pay them, the collection will stay on your credit report, possibly forever! For an example of just how long they can stay on your report, I will share Brian's story with you. He wanted to buy his first house, and his mortgage application was approved, but with one condition. The condition was that he had to pay off a student loan, which had been with a collection company for over 10 years. Brian had no intention of clearing it up, and, as a result, was declined the best rate offer that I had secured for him. My advice to him was to simply pay his student loan debt, as it would restrict his options for years to come if left unpaid.

You may be surprised how many people have collections recorded on their credit reports. Most times, people don't even realize it. They usually find out only when they next apply for some type of financing. The hardest part about finding out that you have a collection reported when you're applying for financing is that it can wreck your chances of approval, or at least cost you higher interest or fees. Note that having a $5 collection can lower your score just as much as a $5,000 one. However, the smaller the collection is, the easier it is for the banks to look past it. Either way, it is something you will want to pay off and clear up as soon as possible, or it will continue to lower your score as long as it is on your report.

Your mortgage payment doesn't always show up on your bureau (credit report), but if you miss enough payments, it could affect the interest rate you're offered from the bank when your mortgage comes up for renewal again. It may even lead to foreclosure proceedings, which is when the bank or lender starts the process of legally taking ownership of your property due to the lack of payments made. Banks or lenders don't want to own your home, but if they aren't getting paid, they will try and sell the property in order to reduce their losses. If you find yourself in a situation where you may not be able to make your mortgage payments, contact your mortgage lender or mortgage agent to find out what can be done. The same thing is true with any creditor. In fact, if you don't think you'll be able to make a payment to any one of your creditors, it is a good rule of thumb to contact them to see if something can be worked out, especially if you contact them before the due date. I've never seen the attitude of pretending it will all go away actually work for anyone.

I understand that despite your best efforts, an emergency may come up, preventing you from being able to make a payment. However, the banks still feel that it is your responsibility to keep track of your accounts and pay your bills on time. Get your head around this rule and you will have a great foundation to always have amazing credit.

Rule 1 – Avergae Joe Action Steps

1. Come up with a system that works for you to either automate your bill payments, or know when each bill payment is due.

2. Consider which accounts you could possibly make multiple payments toward each month.

Chapter 5

Rule 2: High Balances Equal Low Scores

When people hear that they should stay away from high balances, they tend to think about the total amount of money they owe. However, the credit-reporting agencies, TransUnion and Equifax, are more concerned about how much you owe in contrast to what your limit is, also known as loan-to-value (LTV).

Credit-reporting agencies use your LTV, shown as a percentage, as an indicator of how well you manage your credit. So, if you have a limit of $500 on your credit card or line of credit, and your balance owing is $400, your balance is deemed too high. This same $400 balance, with a card limit of $2,000, is considered a low balance.

What exactly makes a high balance?

If you've ever read about credit online or in a book, you may become a bit confused on what actually constitutes a high balance on your credit accounts. Some of these sources state that anything over a 20% limit is deemed a high credit balance. I don't know how that would be practical, as it only allows you to use $200 for every $1,000 of your limit. The TransUnion Canada web site states very clearly that any balance higher than 50% of the limit will harm your credit, and it even suggests aiming for as low as 30% loan-to-value. Based on TransUnion's web site, if your line of credit has a limit of $1,000, every time the bank reports the information to TransUnion, your balance had better be less than $500, or it will lower your credit score. Equifax Canada's new web site doesn't mention any specific ratios. However, its old web site councils us, *"Try not to run your balances up to your credit limit. Keeping your account balances below 75% of your available limit will help your score."*

To get a better understanding of what exactly is classified as a high balance, I pulled the last 100 clients' credit reports to review, and found that any balance less than 50% of their limit didn't make any mention of a high balance. When the balance is between 50% and 75% of its limit, it was mentioned on the report, but it only dropped the score minimally. Scores really starts taking a hit when the loan-to-value ratio or the balance is higher than 75% of the limit. Obviously, the lower the percentage the balances are compared to the limit, the less chance it will have of lowering a client's score. That is why I advise my clients to never use more than half of their limit(s).

One thing everyone seems to agree on is that maxed-out balances or living close to it will drop your score a lot. Plus, it just makes practical sense not to have balances close to their limit, as it will only increase the chances of mistakes being made. If you ever miss a payment, or if you go over your limit, it will drop your score immensely. It doesn't matter if it was a $500 limit or a $50,000 limit, living on or around the limit makes you appear risky to the banks.

Keep in mind that although higher debt amounts don't necessarily lower your score, they could make it harder for you to qualify. However, this is a whole different subject matter for a future book.

I've also met people who claim that because they paid off their balance each time, they didn't feel bad about maxing their credit to the limit during the month. I would not suggest doing this. Lenders report the information electronically to the credit reporting agencies regularly. Even if you pay off the high balance in full, the day after it reports, your credit will still take a hit. Remember, every account has its own payment date and each lender reports to the various reporting agencies at different times. Because of this, it would be impossible to know when it's best to pay the debt down. The trick is to keep your balances low all the time. If you have trouble keeping your balances below 50% of the credit limit on all your credit accounts, then either increase your limits, or move part of the balance to another credit card or line of credit.

Money-saving tip

I have also found it advantageous to have credit established with different banks. This in no way will help increase your credit score; however, it can save you financially to have a history with more than just one bank. For example, I personally have accounts with two of the major banks. The credit card that I have with each of these companies offers special rates for switching balances from one to the other. This trick helps me save money with more than just credit card financing. Banks are more willing to give you their best discounted rates if they can steal some sort of business from a different bank. Competition between lenders assures you that you will get the lowest rates available.

My clients, John and Cathy, who were planning to buy their first home, are good examples of the importance of Rule 2. Although, they had tried to save up enough money for a down payment, they didn't have enough for the typical 5% down. At that time, in 2006, banks had access to a program that offered 100% financing. The kicker was that you had to have a credit score of at least 680. A few months prior to their application for a mortgage, both John and Cathy had credit scores just over the 680 mark, but by the time I pulled their credit report again, it had dropped over 50 points for Cathy and 40 points for John. Even though they had a great repayment history, their last purchase had put them $25 over their $500 limit. As John and Cathy had already picked out the house they wanted and given notice to their landlord, they were now in trouble. The couple looked at getting a co-signer (another applicant brought on to the mortgage to strengthen it) to help, but any willing family members were either not living in the country or not in a position to help. When I spoke to the lenders, they said they couldn't make an exception due to the over-the-limit balance of $25. The two could have easily paid out the debt owing on the card, but because the over-the-limit amount showed up on their credit report, the banks felt they were not in control of their finances and refused to lend them the money. This left John and Cathy no other choice than to continue renting until they could get their credit scores back up to the 680 mark.

Kevin, another one of my clients, learned that although he was approved, not following Rule 2 can be expensive. Although I was able to get the refinancing for his property, he ended up paying a 0.6% higher interest rate, because of his high balances on both his credit cards and loans. I know that an amount less than 1% doesn't seem like much, but for the size of his mortgage, it meant that he would be paying an extra $11,491.41 over five years. One part of Kevin's problem was that he had a lot of credit cards and loans. Although having access to credit or multiple credit cards doesn't necessarily lower your credit score, you have to be organized enough to make sure you're making at least the minimum payment each month. Kevin's repayment history was OK, but because of his life-style, he generally maxed-out his credit at any given time during the month. When I looked at his credit, he had no over-the-limit balances; however, seven of his eight credit accounts had balances over 75% of the credit limit, and four of those were very close, if not at, their limit. He made excellent wages and generally paid his cards off before the end of the month, but the high balances made his credit score much lower. If Kevin's credit score had been just a little bit higher, he would have been approved through a major bank, and his payments would have been considerably lower.

Loans and high balances

In the last couple of examples, I've been talking mostly about credit cards and lines of credit. There is another popular form of credit and that is a loan. Loan balances are much harder to keep at 50% or less of your limit. Think about it: if you apply for a loan, your limit is your balance at day one, and this will lower your score. It is irrelevant to your credit what you paid for the car or how much cash you put for a down payment on your entertainment system. With loans, the lender will only report what your original loan amount was and what your current balance is. It is only until you reach the halfway point of your term that your credit score stops being lowered due to the high balance. If you have the means to qualify for the full amount, and then prepay the balance down to the halfway mark, this would be a great way to build your credit. But unfortunately, the majority of Canadians applying for a loan don't have the resources to prepay a loan more than the minimum set payments.

Some readers may be upset because no one ever warned them about this before. Who would have guessed that Equifax and TransUnion would rank being approved for a new loan as a negative hit to your credit score?

To be honest, there are pros and cons with each type of credit, and I go through these in more detail throughout the book. However, Rule 2 still stands, and you have to realize that with any type of credit, any balance over the halfway mark will lower your credit score.

Rule 2 – Average Joe Action Steps

1. Review your history with your credit accounts and see if you used more than 50% of your credit limits in any of your credit accounts.

2. If you do sometimes go over the 50% mark call your lender and ask if they will auto-increase your limit so you won't go over 50% anymore.

3. If your bank won't increase the limit, see about spreading some of your debt to other accounts.

Chapter 6

Rule 3: You Must Have Established Credit

As important as having a high credit score is, even with an amazing credit score, you can still be declined access to additional credit of any kind. You may be scratching your head wondering why you wouldn't be approved, even though your credit score is soaring. There are two other things that banks look at before they will confirm you have good credit. The first is how long you have had each account established and the second is how high the limits are for each one.

It takes time to build your credit

Think of it this way: to obtain any kind of financing, the lender wants to see if you're going to pay them back. If you have few mistakes on your credit history, the banks will proceed with a bit of caution. But with no history, the banks will find you more risky due to fear of the unknown. If the bank has nothing to rank you on, you either won't be offered their best discounted rates, you will be requested to pay a higher down payment, charged extra fees or be declined.

Before I left for Argentina, I loaned a family member a large sum of money. I based my decision on the fact that I knew she could be trusted. The banks don't actually know you unless you have a prior established relationship. Even if you've dealt with them before for savings or investments, they will still want to see a repayment history when it comes to debt.

The key word for lenders is history. With this family member that I dealt with, I was the bank and I had already established a history with her. No I didn't lend her the money to stop punching me in the arm. I lent her the money because I knew her spending habits; I had witnessed her work ethic while growing up; and I knew she was honest and would keep her word. If she said she was going to pay me back, I knew she would. If I don't know someone and/or can't see their repayment history, there is no way I'd lend my money to them. The banks feel the same way. Unless you are being charged more for rates or fees, no one wants to be the first person to lend you money when you don't have a repayment history.

Secured credit

You may be thinking that if no one wants to be the first, then how is it possible to start building or rebuilding a history? That is an excellent question. The best answer would be to apply for a secured credit card. You can secure the credit card to your house, to investments, or to just plain cash. With a secured credit card $500 is the usual starting limit. This amount can be increased based on other assets and strengths on your application. Secured credit cards are great tools for building or rebuilding your credit. Think of this card exactly like a credit card, but with training wheels. It is attached to your personal name, you get monthly statements, there's a minimum payment, and they are even nice enough to charge you interest.

Unfortunately, in the last couple of years, major banks have made it more apparent that they don't want to issue many secured credit cards. They will still offer them to those people who are young and just starting out, or to those who are new-to-Canada. However, those seeking to rebuild their credit will have to be approved by a non-banking institution. Non-bank lenders, who specialize in dealing with those with bruised credit history, will charge the same interest rate or just slightly higher than that of unsecured credit cards (19% to 24%). The reason the fees and interest rate are similar is because the upfront cash or security minimizes the bank's risk. If you don't make your payments, then eventually they will just take your security deposit. Just remember, if you are late or don't make your payments, your credit will be affected in the same negative way as outlined in Rule 1.

For an up-to-date list of lenders who offer secured credit cards, please visit www.TheAverageJoeBook.com.

Money-saving tip

Some credit companies will allow you to secure a portion of the limit rather than the whole amount. This way you won't have to cough up as much money upfront. For example, it is better to only have to put $300 down as a security on a $500 limit, as this will leave you free to spend the other $200 as you wish. With this scenario, you can then get two credit cards by tying up only $600. I go through the importance of having at least two credit accounts active further on in the chapter. Although it may seem weird to have $600 secured in order to have access to $1,000 of credit, this is where you have to start to establish your credit. As you build a credit history with that company, they will increase your limit, over time, without any more money being required for security.

Please note that there is a difference between a secured credit card and a prepaid one. A prepaid credit card does not improve or harm your credit in any way. It is like a gift card that is paid for in advance and can be used until the total amount is spent. There are no monthly payments, and it doesn't have anyone's name attached to it.

Some Canadians, just starting out, who are 18 or older, have no problem being approved for a credit card. They probably don't have a credit score, but have had some type of banking history with a bank. Due to this fact, they will generally be approved for a student card or some type of basic credit card without too much hassle. Everyone else, including those who are new-to-Canada, will either have to prove an established credit history, or have assets to offset the increased risk for the bank. The good news is that if you get turned down by a major bank, there are usually lots of other options. Just turn on the radio or television and there will always be a lender advertising that your approval will be guaranteed. Most of the time, you don't even have to go looking for one. You will either receive an application in the mail, or be harassed to apply for one at the bank, the mall, the grocery store, or just about anywhere else you can think of!

When re-establishing your credit, car loans will be the easiest form of credit to qualify for. Once again, because the loan is attached to an asset, there is a reduced risk to the lender, so it is more likely that you will be approved.

How long does it take to establish or re-establish your credit?

According to the credit agencies it takes four to five years for each account to be deemed established. TransUnion's web site states, *"The age of the oldest account on your file is a good indicator of how much credit experience you have. If your oldest account is more than four to five years old, you are considered to have solid credit experience. If your oldest credit account is less than that, other factors such as the number of accounts and type of accounts will be more important in determining your ability to manage credit."* (www.transunion.ca). Equifax, as well, confirms that the longer you have an account, the more established your credit appears.

Each bank and lender will have their general approval guidelines, separate from what the credit reporting agencies would consider ideal. Generally, if you have no credit, you will need to establish it for one year before you qualify for mortgage financing. If you have poor credit it will take you at least two years before the major banks will offer you a mortgage. If you are looking to be approved for other types of credit, for example a credit card or a car loan, then your accounts don't have to be established as long before being qualified.

Some readers may be surprised by how short a time it takes for someone to re-establish their credit. Many have the misconception that just because you have bruised credit, you are unable to get approved for any type of credit until it is removed off of your report. That is not the case. To find out exactly how long each type of bruised credit will stay on your credit report, please visit my web site under tools and lists.

Yes, it is true that credit counseling or even bankruptcy will stay on either credit report between two and seven years. However, please keep in mind that the bank and your credit score are almost entirely weighed on the last couple of years, regardless of any previous problems. Also, please note that the clock starts ticking from the time you are either discharged (paid your bankruptcy or credit program in full) or your account has been paid up-to-date.

The point I'm trying to make is that if you are building or rebuilding your credit, it is time to start now. That way, it should only take you between one and two years to have your credit re-established enough to qualify for the best rates once again.

Nick and Melissa are great examples of how two years of re-established credit is the key. Once these clients entered bankruptcy, they began actively seeking education on how to qualify for a mortgage again. Because they received the right information about re-establishing their credit, very early in the process (as soon as they had completed paying for their bankruptcy) they qualified for a 5% down payment and best rates, once again.

If you are considering going bankrupt a second time, please do everything you can to not let that happen. Banks and lenders are less forgiving for people who have previously gone bankrupt. Also Equifax states, "*If the consumer declares several bankruptcies, the system will keep each bankruptcy for fourteen (14) years from the date of each discharge.*"

Please note that no matter what type of financing you apply for, depending on your specific financial situation, you may be able to acquire financing before the usual waiting period is over. However, your interest rates will be much higher and extra fees may be required.

Credit limits and mortgage financing

Mortgage financing is one of the hardest types of financing to get approved for. Unlike business financing, the majority of Canadians will go through mortgage financing multiple times in their lifetime. Banks now want to see that you can handle higher limits on your credit before approving you for a mortgage. This makes sense as the amount the average Canadian is borrowing, especially for mortgages, continues to go up.

So you have always managed a $500-credit limit on your credit card. This is a great start. However, there is a huge difference between missing the $15 minimum monthly payment and a $1,000 or $2,000 monthly payment on a mortgage. That is why, along with a great credit score, the banks are looking for evidence that you can control large amounts of credit.

The banks aren't just referring to having one established account either; they want to see at least two to three. Each of these trade lines (credit accounts such as a credit card, line of credit, or loan from any bank or lender) should have limits of at least $2,500.

Here is how I first learned about how important it is to have higher credit limits. In June 2009, I ran into a situation with my client, Alex, who had one active credit card with a limit of $1,500, and the lender said that it wasn't high enough. I was shocked when I heard that they wanted his limit to be at least $2,500. That condition didn't come from a specific bank either. It came from CMHC, a crown corporation that came into existence mainly to make mortgage money more accessible to the average Canadian. Genworth and Canada Guarantee are both private corporations and competitors with CMHC, but they only own a very small percentage of the market share. Currently, any person who wishes to put less than a 20% down payment on a mortgage needs the approval of any one of these three main insurers. There are banks and lenders that self-insure; they don't go through one of the three major insurers. But these self-insured lenders are generally non-major lenders known as private or B-lenders. These lenders fill the need for those who don't meet the higher requirements of mainstream banks.

The current guidelines being used by the three main insurers, is to have at least a credit limit of $2,500 on two credit accounts in order for someone to have established credit. Because Alex's credit didn't meet CMHC's guidelines, they came back requiring an additional $24,000 in down payment. Luckily, his father was able to give him the extra money, and shortly after that, he increased his limits on his credit cards.

Money-saving tip

When looking for mortgage financing ask a mortgage professional for ways that you can save money with CMHC or any of the other insurers. For example, having a 10% down payment instead of an 8% can save you a couple thousand dollars right off the bat. Other savings can be realized when you reduce your amortization (life of the mortgage) to 25 years or less.

Types of credit that don't build your credit well

One myth that I would like to dispel, and which I'm glad Equifax is also helping to destroy, is that cell phone plans help establish your credit on both reports. If you request your own online Equifax credit report, it will show the cell phone account, but it also notes in the comment section, *"This item is not displayed to all credit grantors and will not impact your score."* On the TransUnion report, most cell phone accounts do show up, and are used to calculate your credit score, but once again, banks won't take it seriously, because the bill payment is generally relatively small.

Another thing to keep in mind is not to use student loans as part of a strategy to build credit. They help you establish a credit score, but if that is all you have reporting on your credit bureau (credit report), banks and lenders won't consider you to have established credit. The reason most lending institutions do not take student loans seriously is because almost anyone can get one. Also, the qualifying is based on how little you make per year, which is the opposite of how the banks qualify you for regular loans and credit.

As well intended as any advice may be, you have to be careful what information you trust. I have parents calling me all the time saying that they would like their son or daughter to qualify for a mortgage in order to build their credit. Not that this is a bad thing, but mortgages don't build your credit score. Although a mortgage can show up on your credit bureau (credit report), and the address of the property is usually stamped on your report, it doesn't build your score. Equifax confirms this on their reports. They say, *"Mortgage information may appear in your credit report, but is not used to calculate your credit score."*

If you have a home equity line of credit (line of credit attached to your house) instead, or combined with a mortgage, most likely it will show up on your credit bureau because the majority of lending institutions will report it. All mortgages with good repayment histories will help you build a relationship with the current institution that holds that mortgage. However, it won't help your credit score.

The previous couple of examples won't always help build your credit, but they can hurt it. For example, if you don't pay your cell phone bill or make your mortgage payment as scheduled, the lender will eventually send the cell phone bill to a collections company, or put your mortgage into foreclosure, which will really hurt your credit.

Rule 3 – Average Joe Action Steps

1. If you haven't started building or rebuilding your credit, get a plan in place and start now.

2. If you don't already have at least two credit accounts with limits of $2,500 each, get them!

3. If you are using mortgages, cell phones or student loans to try and build your credit – repeat the second action step.

Chapter 7

Rule 4: Some Types of Credit Are Better Than Others

Many of my clients ask me which bank or which type of credit is better. My answer is, it depends on you. There are three major things to consider before deciding. First, be very honest with yourself. Look at the pros and cons and see which option will help you achieve active and established credit, but also won't get you further into debt. For example, if a credit card with a limit of $2,500 or higher will get you into trouble, then it's just not worth having. If you're just maintaining a loan in order to keep your credit active, try an investment loan, so at least you will be increasing your financial position while you're improving your credit. Talk to your financial planner for further details on investment loans and if they are right for you.

Second, compare the selling features of each option, as some may have a bit of a higher interest rate, but allow you more flexibility. And third, READ THE FINE PRINT. Just because you get an introductory rate or reward points, it may not be worth the yearly fees. Unfortunately, as consumers, we get so caught up in one feature that we don't take the time to understand what the costs associated with it are. As the old adage states, "To be forewarned, is to be forearmed."

My objective in this section isn't to tell you which bank or lender is better, rather, it is to explain the different types of credit available to you, as well as their pros and cons. The three different types of credit accounts are: Revolving, Installments, and Open.

REVOLVING (R) ACCOUNTS:

Revolving Credit Accounts include credit cards and lines of credit (unsecured or secured to assets such as property, investments, or cash). The payment fluctuates depending on the interest rate, the balance owing, and the type of account you have.

The pros of revolving credit

I like revolving accounts because you can pay them down and reuse them whenever you want to. This is very helpful if you need money for a short-term period. You can use what you need and then pay it down again as soon as you get paid or the money becomes available. The payments are generally lower than that of an Installment (loan) type account because it is common for them to have interest-only or low payment requirements. If you have interest-only payments, then you will never pay the debt off, unless you make additional contributions to the account. Even Revolving accounts that include a balance paydown portion in your payments, will still take years to pay down your debt. For example, on a credit card balance of $5,000, you are looking at around 40 years to pay it down to $0, when just making your minimum payments.

Credit cards: My favourite part about credit cards is that the only time you pay interest on them is when you don't pay your monthly balance off in full each month. This allows you the convenience of using the card and always keeping your credit active, without being forced to pay any interest at all. If you travel a lot, they are great to have, and of course, there are reward points on most cards.

Lines of credit: If you carry debt from month to month, I suggest that a line of credit would be better for you. The interest rate that you will be charged will be much less than that of credit cards. Although a line of credit is not as flexible as a credit card, you can still transfer money from account to account instantly.

Secured lines of credit: This type of credit is exactly the same as a line of credit, but, because they are attached or secured to some kind of asset, such as a house or investment, your interest rate is usually a bit lower. There are also some banks who will give you a debit card with this account, which helps you have easy access to your credit. Depending on the worth of the asset, you can also have larger limits. This is because, if you don't make your payments, the lender can take your asset to cover the balance of the debt.

The cons of revolving credit

Temptation! Although ease of access is one of the pros to revolving credit, for those of us without strong will power, it could become a problem. The combination of ease of access and low minimum payments are just too much for some people. Just read the financial section of any newspaper and you will find out that Canadians are going further and further into debt. Revolving credit is not the problem; it is that there is a lack of education when it comes to money and being responsible with your credit.

Credit cards: Annual fees. A lot of times, in exchange for more points or to be offered a lower interest rate, credit card companies may charge you an annual fee. I don't suggest that you go this route because you can get rewards cards without paying fees, and if you are carrying balances, you should use a line of credit instead.

Lines of credit: Daily compounding interest means that from the moment you have a balance, you will be charged interest on a daily basis. In other words, for a very short-term debt, it will be cheaper to utilize your credit cards. For example, you have planned a vacation away to a tropical destination and you have to pay for it now to reserve the booking. If you don't have all the money right now but you will shortly, it would be better to pay for it with a credit card than with your line of credit. With the credit card, you will be charged interest-only if you don't pay off the full amount before your billing date. With the line of credit, even though the interest rate isn't as high as the credit card, the interest charged is based on the balance of each day.

Secured lines of credit: Even more temptation! Many people find themselves in trouble because, unlike a credit card or line of credit that generally has a limit of $10,000 or less, it is not uncommon to see secured credit with limits of $100,000 plus. That is more than most people make in a year. Just to clarify, it isn't the higher limit amount that is bad, rather, it is that there is more temptation to utilize higher debt amounts. The more debt you have, the higher your minimum monthly payment will be.

INSTALLMENT (I) ACCOUNTS

Every types of loan falls under the category of installment accounts (I). Your payment is based on a set term that has part interest and part principle paydowns. Unlike revolving credit, you can't take out any more money on the loan, unless you go through the application and approval process first.

The pros of using installment accounts:

When using this type of account, it takes a conscious decision to get into more debt, in addition to being approved by a lender to increase your balance(s). Loan payments will have a term associated with them. A term is the maximum length of time it will take you to pay off the loan (except with mortgages), based on the interest rate, payment schedule, and the terms and conditions found in your contract. This means there is a light at the end of the tunnel; any extra payments you make above and beyond your minimum required amount will simply shorten the length of the loan.

Personal loan: The nice thing about a personal loan is that you don't have to secure it to anything. It can be used to consolidate debt or to buy something that is not an asset.

Secured loan: Car and investment loans, along with mortgages, fall under this category. Generally, the interest rate will be better, and it is easier to qualify for because of reduced risk to the lending institution. Remember, mortgages, even if they show up on your credit report, do not build your credit. No one has ever been able to give me a good reason why a mortgage loan doesn't build your credit score, but currently it doesn't.

The cons of installment accounts:

The biggest reason why I personally don't like to use loans when accessing credit is because 99% of the time, you are forced to pay some type of interest. There are generally application or administration fees involved in order to set up or even close an installment account. As discussed in Rule 2, loans are harder to keep the balance at 50% or less of your limit. Generally, once you have been approved for a loan, your balance is your limit, and your score will be lowered because of it. With each payment you make, it will lessen the impact on your credit, until you are about halfway through your term. At this point, the loan will start to improve your credit again.

Personal loans: They are a bit harder to qualify for and they come with a higher interest rate than secured loans.

Secured loan: Although the loan interest rates are lower than credit cards, sometimes, there are restrictions to making extra payments. In most situations, however, paying a slightly higher interest rate is worth having the flexibility of an early repayment option.

OPEN (O) ACCOUNT

The web site (consumer.ic.gc.ca) for the Office of Consumer Affairs (OAC) defines "O" as being, *"open credit such as a line of credit, where you can borrow money as needed, up to a certain limit, and the total balance is due at the end of each period. This category may also include student loans, for which the money may not become due until you are out of school."*

Please ignore the definition and examples used in the OAC web site as quoted above. An open account is simply a credit card or an account; you can borrow money as needed and the total balance is due at the end of each period, generally monthly. For those readers who were around before credit cards became popular, it may be helpful to think of an (O) account as a charge card or Diners Card. For those of you scratching your head because you have never heard of such cards, let me use a different example. Cell phone accounts today are a far more commonly found type of "O" account.

Pros of (O) Open accounts:

Although, open credit is very different from the revolving type, it shares the benefit of convenience. It looks and acts the same as any credit card that allows you the flexibility to buy/use what you want when you want it. The other main benefit is that you don't have a limit. Think of this type of credit like the Autobahns (Freeways) in Germany, which posts a "recommended speed" of 130 km/h but there is no actual speed limit.

Charge cards: Using a charge card instead of a revolving credit card would allow you to discard Rule 2! The reason you could disregard Rule 2 on any (O) type account is because it is impossible to utilize more than 50% of your limit, when there is no limit. This would be a good option for those of you who put large amounts on your credit card, but faithfully pay it off at the end of each month.

Cell phone accounts: There are a couple of benefits to having a cell phone contract, as opposed to a prepaid contract. First, there are only a few types of prepaid cell phones so your selection is limited. The second benefit is that you don't have to go run out to a corner store to buy more minutes. This way you will never miss a phone call or a Facebook update just because you have gone over the agreed minimum amounts that you originally signed up for. It can also be an inexpensive way to get your credit started, as well as an easy way to qualify. Of course, as we learned in the previous chapter, it won't help you have established credit; however, it is a start.

Cons of (O) Open accounts

Charge cards: If you think an interest rate between 18% to 24% is bad, try the typical 30% if you don't pay your charge card balance off in full each month. Not only are you charged the high interest rate, but there is no such thing as a minimum payment. This means that if the balance isn't paid off 100% each month, it will be registered as a late payment. That is why (O) accounts are very rare and most credit card companies and banks don't even offer them.

Cell phone accounts: As previously discussed, a cell phone account currently will not improve your credit score with Equifax, although it shows up on your report. However, with TransUnion, the other major credit-reporting agency in Canada, it does appear on your credit report, and it will affect your credit score.

You may have heard from some "credit gurus" that it is really important to have all types of credit, such as loans, revolving credit, and open credit, in order to establish good credit. Both of the reporting agencies, Equifax and TransUnion, allude to this commonly misunderstood statement on their web sites. TransUnion's web site (www.transunion.ca) says that, *"A healthy credit profile has a balanced mix of credit accounts and loans."* Equifax also makes a brief reference to this on some of their personal credit reports. They state that, *"Generally the more diversified in industry and types of accounts you have, the higher your score is."*

When I first read this, I couldn't believe it. I, personally, had only used revolving accounts, such as credit cards and lines of credit, in order to start and maintain a high credit score. It worked for me, so I have been advising clients for years to try and stick with revolving credit alone. The only time I suggested using installment or open accounts was when a client knew that the easy access to revolving credit would be too tempting for them to handle correctly or other special circumstances. So, I decided to test the credit reporting statements to find out exactly how important it was to have different types of credit on your report.

For this experiment, I compared a large amount of credit reports that I had already reviewed with my mortgage clients. I used only the best reports; those without missing payments, collections, or non-established credit histories on them. After reviewing the top 100 credit reports, here are the results. Any credit report with a score over 800, which is really good, had only one type of credit on them, and all of these clients used revolving credit to maintain their excellent credit.

Just to be clear, just because the credit reports I reviewed had loans and open accounts on them does not mean they didn't have good credit. Most of them were between the 750 to 799 mark, which is still great. I used this example above to illustrate that having a variety of different credit accounts can improve your score, but it isn't necessary in order to have well-established credit.

On applications, lenders only review your repayment history. They are not concerned whether the type of credit you are using is a credit card or a car loan. This means that you need to find out which method of credit best for you. Follow the Nine Rules of Credit, and you will be good to go!

HELOC vs. Mortgage

I am constantly asked if home equity lines of credit (HELOC) are a good choice, and my answer again would be, it all depends. You need to review the pros and cons of each type of credit and decide which will help you best achieve your financial goals. I would also suggest you talk with a mortgage professional, first, as part of the process of educating yourself on both options. This may help with your decision-making, as I believe that there are advantages and dis-advantages to both.

Below are some questions I ask clients who are interested in switching from a typical mortgage loan to a HELOC. It is important to answer these questions honestly.

If you had an extra $400 each month, because you now have interest-only payments, would you do any of the following:

- Move into a bigger home?
- Eat out more?
- Vacation more?
- Buy a newer vehicle?
- Spend it on your kids?
- Buy more stuff?

If you answered yes to either of these questions, I would suggest that you stay away from home equity lines of credit. If you answered no to the above questions, and it makes sense financially, go for it.

Credit Consolidation Trap

Please be aware that there is a very real danger of any one of us falling into the credit consolidation trap. We may start off with good intentions, but when it comes to finances, we seem to have short-term memories. Consolidating debt is when you take all of your debt and try and put it together under one account. Not only does this typically put your balances over 50% of the limit, but it can also hurt you in other ways.

Consolidating all the balances and freeing up some cash flow, or limits on other cards, can make it all too tempting to get into a bit more debt.

One way people consolidate debt is with balance transfers. These are low introductory rate offers that are only good for a limited time, like six months to a year. Before you get too excited when you see the advertising of 1.9% or 3.9% being offered, be aware; there is some fine print. If you don't pay your card off in full at the expiry of the offer, your rates will jump from single digits to double digits, which are generally higher than your original interest rate. Remember, the banks are in the business of making money, and they are offering a "special rate" to you because they are hoping that you will be like the majority of their clients, who either don't pay their balance off, or go and get into a bunch more debt because the interest rate is so low.

The goal of credit consolidation is to get your debt changed over to accounts that have low interest rates. The most common medium for consolidation seems to be with mortgage financing. The rates are lower due to the fact that the credit account is secured with a house, and so people mix their personal consumer debt with a mortgage or a HELOC. There is nothing wrong with doing this, and if you look at the numbers, it generally makes financial sense. The problem with this is that it is too easy. The habits that put you in that situation in the first place, most likely, haven't changed. Therefore, once you have successfully grouped the debt together, and lowered your payments, what are you tempted to do? Go shopping!

Unfortunately, there seems to be more "shopaholic" in us than most of us want to admit. If you have read the Shopaholic series of books written by Sophie Kinsella, or watched the movie, "Confessions of a Shopaholic," you may be able to identify with the main character. This series follows Becky Bloomwood, a woman in her early 30s, who can't help but shop; it becomes her retail form of therapy. There is nothing wrong with credit consolidation, but there is a real danger if it is used to temporally relieve a guilty conscience, or make room for new purchases on your credit. Unlike the movie, debt or the unintentional desire to abuse credit, doesn't just disappear because you've found your soulmate, no matter how dreamy or rich he is.

Rule 4 – Average Joe Action Steps

1. Honestly review how you've handled certain types of credit or money, and find out which type of credit works best for you.

2. If you are thinking of consolidating your debt, ask yourself first, "Have I changed the action that got me into debt in the first place?" If not, change what is causing the problem first and then look at consolidation as an option. If you don't know how to change, go to www.TheAverageJoeBook.com for info and links on better money management.

Chapter 8

Rule 5: What You Don't Use, You Lose!

The average Joe may think that once you've established your credit and you have a high score that you're good to go. The problem is that the credit reporting agencies who decide how each rule is weighed aren't the average Joe. This is how Equifax and TransUnion see it: No matter what type of credit account you use to establish your history, they want it kept active. If you stop using your accounts, they will eventually be deemed inactive. Inactive accounts don't lower your score at all; they just stop improving your credit. Think of your credit like walking up the down escalator. At any point during the journey if you stop moving forward, you are eventually going to end up at the bottom again.

For those of you who are just starting to establish credit or rebuilding your credit, loans have one advantage I didn't mention in the previous chapter. They force you to pay, at least once each month. During the length of your loan, it is those payments that help keep that account established and active. The downside is that the moment you make your last payment, on any type of loan, it is no longer considered active. This statement may take the average Joe by surprise; I know it did me. I thought that a loan showing paid in full would enhance my credit rating. However, it doesn't. Although, it won't hurt your credit either, but each credit account, no matter what type it is, has to show as current in order for it to count. Below are examples on where to look on your own credit reports to find out the last time that each of your accounts was used.

Equifax Example

Car Loan Ltd.

Phone Number:	(905) 321-1119	**High Credit/Credit Limit**	0000006936
Account Number:	XXX....285	**Payment Amount:**	$144.00
Association in Account:	Joint	**Balance:**	$7,161.00
Type of Account:	Installment	**Past Due:**	$2,312.00
Date Opened:	2007-02	**Date of Last Activity:**	**2009-10**
Status:	Closed by Consumer		
		Date Reported:	2010-10
Months Reviewed:	No payment 30 days late		
Payment History:	No payment 60 days late		
	No payment 90 days late		

TransUnion Example

Your Bank

Account #:	****123	**Type:**	Type: Revolving Account	**Opened:**	08/17/2005
Condition:	(Open)	**Pay:**	Paid as Agreed	**Reported:**	**02/04/2012**
Balance:	....	**Status:**	Satus: Open	**Responsibility:**	Individual
High Balance:	$10,000	**Payment:**	$0 Monthly (due every		Account
Terms			month)	**Past Due:**	
		Limit:			

Remarks: Line of Credit
Amt In High Credit Column (Disp 122–130 of Trade Segment) is Credit Limit
Two Year Payment History:

TransUnion OK OK OK OK OK OK OK OK OK OK OK OK OK OK OK OK OK OK OK OK OK OK OK OK
          feb mar apr may jun jul aug sep oct nov dec 11 feb mar apr may jun jul aug sep oct nov dec 12

Six Year Payment History:

30 Days Late: 0   60 Days Late: 0   90 Days Late: 0

Here is an example I used earlier in my book that illustrates the bank's position on loans. In Rule 3, I told you the story of Alex and how CMHC required him to put another $24,000 toward his down payment before he could be approved for his mortgage financing. CMHC decided this was necessary because they said he had weak credit. In addition to Alex's one active credit card, he also had several other loans or installment accounts; they just weren't active. He had a car and an RSP loan that he had previously paid off, one only two months beforehand. Like the average Joe, Alex thought that it would show better to the banks if the loans was paid. Alex guessed wrong, and because of that he had to pay the price, double the amount of down payment he wanted to put down.

A downside to revolving credit accounts, such as a credit card, is that you have to keep track of how often it gets used. However, the advantage is that the account doesn't ever have to be closed or paid off. It can remain at a zero balance for a while and still be deemed active.

My suggestion would be to use your revolving credit at least once every four to six months in order to keep it active.

If you have a hard time controlling revolving credit, I would suggest that you develop a plan to keep yourself from being able to access it too easily. For example, you can literally freeze your credit cards by storing your credit cards in a block of ice in your freezer. If you do try this, make sure you put a reminder on the calendar to thaw them out and use them occasionally. The balance doesn't have to be there long, but it will appear on your credit report. This will keep that account active, and then you can continue using cash or a different credit account for most of your expenses. If you have a parent or partner who you trust, you could also ask them to hold onto the credit card or hide it from you until a specific date. That way you can protect yourself from the temptation of easy access and still keep your credit active. For other types of revolving accounts, like lines of credit. You should stay away from these types until you have more will power.

A professor at one of the universities I taught a credit semi-nar at shared this experience with me. After finishing his schooling and establishing his credit, this teacher received a job offer in the United States, which he accepted. He lived in the US for a couple of years. When he came back to Canada, he couldn't get approved for a mortgage at his bank, even though he had a good, secure job lined up. While in the US, he hadn't kept his Canadian credit active, so his credit rating showed up as an R instead of a number. An R credit score is a reject beacon, which basically tells potential lenders that there is not sufficient active information or history to provide a score.

Don't confuse this R credit score with an (R) for a revolving credit account. It is often better to have some late payments show up on your history than not have any active payments. Underwriters (the people who decide whether or not your financing will be approved) understand that things happen in life and that there may be good rea-sons why payments were tardy. Therefore, they will often look past these things. But with no repayment history to examine, it makes it very difficult for someone to be approved for any type of financing. There is no information to determine whether you are the type of person who makes your payments on time, or someone who doesn't make them at all!

The professor had to rent a house for six months before he found a bank that would overlook his newly re-established credit history. Most lending institutions will allow you to use international credit reports as established credit for mortgage financing. However, not all banks accept other forms of credit records in lieu of a Canadian credit report. Also, not every country has a credit-reporting agency, as we do in Canada. Even if they do, you would need to obtain a copy of your report in a format that an underwriter in Canada could understand.

You don't have to leave the country for your credit to go inac-tive. Recently, I had a couple looking for mortgage financing and found that everything about their credit was great. It was well-established, bills were paid on time, and they had credit scores over 700. I thought the deal would be a slam dunk. Upon further examination, I noticed that the main applicant, Jake, hadn't used any of his credit over the last eight months. After talking to Emily, his wife, I found out that he travels to remote areas for work seven days at a time, and when he does comes home; he just has a day or two to relax with the family before leaving again. In the meantime, Emily had been making all the purchases and controlling the finances for the family, but only using her own credit cards. This made Jake's credit accounts inactive. This was a concern for the underwriter, because all the family income was generated by Jake, yet his credit remained inactive. I fully explained their circumstances to the underwriter, but she still requested some additional bills with Jake's name on them. Jake needed to show six months of statements from two other bills, with his name on them, just to prove he actively paid his bills on time. This couple was happy to get the mortgage rate they wanted through a major bank; however, they weren't so thrilled about the extra paperwork required.

No matter what type of financing you're looking for, nothing, and I mean nothing, is better than having a well-established credit score and an active credit history.

Rule 5 – Average Joe Action Steps

1. If building/rebuilding, use your credit at least once a month, If just maintaining your credit, use every four to six months, at a minimum.

2. Review your credit and if you only have loans for established credit, look at opening revolving accounts to protect yourself from having to restart your credit over with each loan.

3. If you are planning on leaving the country for more than six months, make sure you keep your credit active while you are away.

Chapter 9

Rule 6: Be Careful With Joint Credit

I was taught to always include my spouse in all our financial decisions. However, I've now learned that "joint credit" is something to stay away from until after your credit has been established. As you and your partner decide what works best for you, here is something to keep in mind. Each person must build his or her own credit and keep it active as long as they live.

The pros of joint credit

Please don't misinterpret my warnings about the dangers of joint credit as meaning that holding credit together is always a bad thing. Joint credit can be a great tool. For example, it is common for one partner to utilize their credit more than another. Joint credit can help keep each partner's credit active, which would have really helped Emily and Jake's situation. If you remember that previous example from Rule 5, Jake didn't use his credit at all, but if they would have had joint credit, his wife, who managed the family finances, could have kept it active for him. This would have allowed them to qualify for their mortgage financing much more easily. It is crucial to always keep both your individual and your joint accounts active. That way you won't have any credit issues in this area.

The cons of joint credit

Let me share another example, from one of my clients, to better illustrate the importance of how joint credit can hurt you. After Melanie got married, Jordan, her husband worked and provided for her and their family. Melanie stopped working outside of the home, and had her name added to Jordan's credit cards. She wasn't the primary applicant on any credit accounts anymore. Everything was great until Jordan suddenly passed away. Going through the normal grieving process was bad enough, but to add to Melanie's devastation, she was declined when she tried to access some of the equity in their house. Equity is the difference between what the house is worth and how much is still owed on the mortgage. Melanie was told by the bank that she couldn't have access to any new funds because she had no active credit showing up on either of her TransUnion or Equifax reports. It didn't matter if she was the one writing the cheques or paying the bills. Without a credit score, the banks had no active history under her name showing that she had been able to make payments on time or at all.

The average Joe may reason that surely the lenders would make an exception in the instance of the death of a spouse. However, the bank did not make an exception, and this is why. From their perspective, whoever's name is on the bill is the one responsible for paying it. For the banks, it is impossible to try to guess who's paying the bill. Due to the lack of credit, Melanie now required a co-signer. This is another person who is financially stable and added to the mortgage application to obtain the extra finances needed.

Another option we could have used is to apply to what is called a private or B-lender. These types of non-traditional lenders require less documentation and will make more exceptions on a case such as Melanie's. The downside to using these lenders, though, is that they usually offer higher interest rates and charge extra fees.

I also had a personal experience that illustrates how the dangers of credit aren't isolated to just a husband and wife relationship. Before I went to South America, I had my father added to my credit card as a co-applicant. What I didn't know was that although they issued my dad his own card, it was still my account, as I was the primary applicant. I would have been held responsible for everything my dad bought with his card, and had he not made his payments, it would have only affected my credit, not his. Initially, I thought adding my father to my credit account was a great way to keep my credit active while I was out of the country, but there was also a huge risk involved. What if my dad had decided to run off to Mexico with some pretty little señorita? Making even the minimum payments would have been the last thing on his mind. Although my dad had a separate card, with a different credit card number, and only his name on it, I would have been held entirely responsible for any debt acquired.

Both of the above experiences are examples of when joint credit can be dangerous to your credit. In Melanie's case, although she paid the bills, because she didn't have anything in her name, it limited her options when Jordan passed away. In my situation, because I had added another person onto the original account, and we didn't apply at the same time, good or bad it would only affect my credit and not my dad's. In addition, my dad would not be building his credit even if he was the one making the payments on time.

Let me clarify something here. Credit agencies and banks have never looked negatively on one's credit just because they have joint accounts; you just have to understand how to use joint credit properly. In order to do this, you need to know how each account is registered. The absolute only way of knowing how an account is reporting is by verifying it yourself. As knowledgeable as family, friends, and even some sales reps are, you need to see it for yourself. To get copies of credit reports for both yourself and your joint account holder, go to www.TheAverageJoeBook.com for the links to each credit-reporting agency.

The following examples show how you can tell if an account is joint with someone else or individually owned.

Equifax Example

Car Loan Ltd.

Phone Number:	(905) 321-1119	**High Credit/Credit Limit**	0000006936
Account Number	XXX....285	**Payment Amount:**	$144.00
Association to Account	Joint ◄———	**Balance:**	$7,161.00
Type of Account:	Installment	**Past Due:**	$2,312.00
Date Opened:	2009-04	Date of Last Activity:	2009-10
Status	Open	**Date Reported:**	2010-10
Months Reviewed:	No payment 30 days late		
Payment History	No payment 60 days late		
	No payment 90 days late		

TransUnion Example

Your Bank

Account #:	****123	**Type:**	Type: Revolving Account	**Opened:**	08/17/2005	
Condition:	(Open)	**Pay:**	Paid as Agreed	Reported:	02/04/2012	
Balance:	....	**Status:**	Status: Open	**Responsibility:**	Individual	
High Balance:	$10,000	**Payment:**	$0 Monthly (due every		Account	
Terms			month)	**Past Due:**		
		Limit:				

Remarks: Line of Credit

Amt In High Credit Column (Disp 122–130 of Trade Segment) is Credit Limit

Two Year Payment History:

TransUnion OK OK OK OK OK OK OK OK OK OK OK OK OK OK OK OK OK OK OK OK OK OK OK OK
feb mar apr may jun jul aug sep oct nov dec 11 feb mar apr may jun jul aug sep oct nov dec 12

Six Year Payment History:

30 Days Late: 0   60 Days Late: 0   90 Days Late: 0

Another reason to be cautious with joint credit is just in case the nature of your relationship changes. For example, when a marriage ends in divorce, it doesn't matter who spent the money. If the debt is registered on both of your credit reports, you are, individually, held 100% responsible for paying it off and making sure the minimum payment is taken care of.

So, if your only credit account is shared jointly with someone else, and you have to cancel that credit, or if the minimum payment is not met, you now have to start from square one. That is why it is important for both partners to have established, active credit separate from one another.

It is also very common, when a couple separates or divorces, that one or both parties discontinue making payments on their debt. Some stop making the minimum payment because they feel it isn't their responsibility anymore and others because their lawyers have told them to forego further payments. The downside to this is that even if you are officially divorced, you can't cancel or take your name off the account until either it is paid down to zero, or unless ordered so by the courts. You can try and freeze the account, but that doesn't always work. You can freeze your account by calling in a lost/stolen card or by asking the bank to verify if they will put a hold on the account. Even if a judge eventually rules in your favour about whose debt it really is, in the meantime, your personal credit will be messed up.

Some types of financing, such as mortgage financing, won't even allow you to use someone else's income on an application, unless they have established credit. This means that once again, you may not qualify for the full amount of money that you need, or you may be charged a higher interest rate, because one of you didn't have your credit established.

It is common for both men and women to take paternity and maternity leaves from work. So, what happens if your mortgage is up for renewal or you are applying for financing, and someone is on paternity or maternity leave or if one of you is out of work? How are you going to qualify for financing if one of you doesn't have established credit? If you both have strong established credit, you will have many more options to keep you in the best financial position possible.

Here is a personal example on why both partners in a relationship should have established credit. My wife Jess stays at home and works very hard teaching and trying to keep our two very energetic toddlers from reeking havoc on our house. She doesn't have a job outside of the home, but Jess helps my business with bookkeeping and other paperwork. She also has a couple of smaller, home-based businesses that she works on part-time. Not only does she contribute to the family by raising our kids, but she also adds to the family income.

Now, with our third bouncing bundle of joy in the oven, and needing more room to transport goods for one of her businesses, Jess needs what she refers to as a "Swagger Wagon." I guess that's a cooler way of saying minivan. Having followed the Nine Rules of Credit since our marriage began, she was automatically approved for a car loan when she went in to meet with someone at the bank. She was in and out of the bank within 20 minutes, which is record timing with two toddlers in tow.

By getting the new vehicle on her own, Jess's action will be a huge help to me in the future when I may require more business or personal financing, as I won't have to include this purchase on my application. This in turn will allow me to be approved for a larger loan amount. It is also beneficial to have two incomes listed on an application, in order to help you qualify for higher loans, or possibly even lower interest rates.

Money-saving tip

If you have one partner with good credit and the other with bad credit, try applying under only the name of the partner that has good credit. This will get you a lower interest rate, and thus save you money. However, this won't work if the person with bad credit earns all the money, and the person who has good credit doesn't. Talk to your mortgage professional or credit rep to see what your options are.

Death, divorce, and babies aren't the only things that can turn your financial life upside down. Life is always full of surprises, and you'll be thankful you were prepared for these times by following my advice. In short, I strongly advise everyone to have at least two personal credit accounts, because you never know what could happen to your partner. Then, in addition to your personal credit, you can apply for some joint credit accounts, if you think it would help keep each other's accounts more active.

Rule 6 – Average Joe Action Steps

1. Review your credit reports to make sure you know how each credit account is reporting, joint or single.

2. If you don't have at least two credit accounts just in your name, make it happen.

Chapter 10

Rule 7: Applying for Credit Lowers Your Score

I am glad to see many more of my clients asking about this rule before they give their consent for a credit check. On your credit report, you will see the names of any one person or company who has checked your credit report. Some of these inquiries lower your score and some don't. Hard inquires are made by commercial institutions, and not only do they lower your score, but other lenders will be able to see the names of these creditors. Soft inquires don't lower your score and can't be seen by other creditors.

The exact number by which your score lowers due to a hard inquiry will depend on numerous factors, but generally it will be somewhere between five and ten points. Many people don't understand why just checking their score will lower it. The credit reporting agencies, both Equifax and TransUnion, view the loss of five to ten points as something that won't make or break your credit, so they are not too concerned. However, credit reporting agencies make it very clear that they want to discourage people from applying for new credit regularly.

That is why there is a practice of detracting points for a certain pattern of credit checks. Equifax confirms this fact on their web site by saying, *"Even if you're just comparison-shopping for the best rate, too many inquiries can be viewed as a desperate bid to obtain credit to get out of financial trouble."* (www.equifax.ca) TransUnion explains it this way: *"Each hard inquiry may cause a drop in your credit score. Multiple inquiries within a short amount of time, such as when you are shopping for a mortgage, are grouped together to lessen the impact. The actual impact depends on the number of inquiries, time period, and other factors on your credit profile."* (www.transunion.ca)

Due to the reporting agencies' vague explanations, everyone seems to have a different opinion on the matter. Some say that any number of inquiries for the same type of financing within 30-days counts as one hit, and some say each application will negatively affect your score. Everyone else seems to be somewhere in the middle, believing that you have a few days' grace between inquiries. However, according to the two explanations above, we can draw the following conclusions: With Equifax, it seems to come down to the number of inquiries made rather than the time frame. With TransUnion, they do mention grouping similar inquires; but this seems to be done only to lessen the impact rather than to completely take away the consequence of lowering a credit score.

After testing these theories on both my own Equifax and TransUnion reports, in addition to reviewing those of my clients, I have come to the following conclusions. A single inquiry will affect your credit score similarly on both reports. Equifax seems to group multiple credit inquiries from the same institution, rather than by industry, as one, as long as they are made within a short time frame. When I tested it on my credit report, the four inquires that I made within the same week, and by the same company, lowered my score by six points. TransUnion reports seem to have a bit longer grace period, and are okay with grouping similar inquiry requests as one, even if they are not from the same company. To pinpoint the exact loss caused by multiple inquires is difficult, and my best advice is to try to avoid credit inquiries at all times, except when reviewing your own credit.

Multiple credit checks can also hurt your chances of being approved in ways other than by lowering your credit score. Some banks, especially for mortgages, may see recent inquiries as an indicator that you have new debt out there that has not yet been reported. For example, if you have had multiple credit checks from banks and car companies, and now you are applying for a mortgage, the new lender may question if you have bought a car that won't show up on your credit report for another 15 to 30 days. The more you owe, the higher the risk you are to the banks. If lenders deem you too risky, they may charge you fees, higher interest rates, or even worse, turn you down. If a lot of inquiries for the same type of financing show up on your report, lending institutions may think you can't be approved elsewhere. If multiple companies have denied you, then why should another one accept you? Obviously, they will look at other key components, but it may cause the underwriter to take a closer look at your file.

I, like most people, don't see rate-shopping as a bad thing, because most of the time we're just trying to get the best possible financing package. It doesn't matter what type of financing you are applying for, whether it's the lowest rate for a credit card, a car loan, or mortgage financing, a hard credit inquiry will affect your credit the same way.

In order to eliminate the risk of your score dropping with this rule; you can always pull your own credit report, make copies, and give one to everyone who needs one. This lets you and the sales rep know exactly what you look like on paper, and it doesn't affect your score. You can personally request your credit report as many times as you want to, and it won't register your name on the list of inquiries or have any other negative affect.

Here are a couple of examples on how making copies of your personal credit report can help in real-life situations. Let's say you're looking to buy a new car and want the best financing possible. Having your credit report in front of them will allow the lender to make a preliminary assessment on what amount they can offer you. However, if you should decide to go ahead with the financing, they will have to access your credit report for themselves. Although you will still have to get your credit checked, you can do all the shopping around you want before it lowers your score.

You can also use this system with mortgage financing. If you only know your score, a mortgage specialist can only give you a rough estimate of the best rate the banks may offer you, but a copy of your credit report, along with the score, will allow any mortgage professional to better know what you will qualify for. They should also be able to analyze the strengths and weaknesses of your credit report and advise you of any concerns a bank may have and how to resolve them.

The one type of financing I have not seen this method of pre-pulling your report work for is with credit cards. Most major banks, and even the small department stores, will ask you to call a toll-free number to apply. You can ask them to quote you their interest rates before you apply, but the general rule is that they won't talk to you until they look at your credit.

Money-saving tip

Call your credit card company to ask them if they can lower your rate. Most people have a hard time believing that credit card rates are negotiable. A number of years ago, I attended a real-estate investment seminar with about 90 other people. One day, our homework was to call our credit card companies and just ask them if we could get our rates lowered. I made the call and was surprised when they lowered mine from 19% to 12%. I thought I had done an awesome job! The next morning, I found out that about half of the class, who had also called their credit card companies, had similar positive results. I was really surprised to hear that some reported being able to get their rates down as low as 6.5%, and not just temporarily, as with a balance transfer either. Since that seminar, I have called my credit card companies and discovered that if you mention that you have just received an offer from a competing credit card company, it will help you negotiate an even better interest rate with your existing credit card provider. If you want a benchmark rate to work off of, you can always look on the Internet to check out rates of other credit card companies, or even rates that your same company is offering to others. Usually, credit card companies will advertise low rates to get more new customers, so you can use this to help you negotiate a lower interest rate. The worst they can do is say no, and then you either continue with the same rate, or you try a different bank to see who will give you the best rate and terms.

No matter what type of financing you are applying for, knowing the strength of your credit will give you peace of mind. It can also help you negotiate the best terms and conditions for your next financing package with confidence.

Read before you sign

Any time that you are asked to sign a contract, read the entire document over carefully, especially the fine print. Even if you don't think a credit check is required for what you're applying for, it's always good to verify it. Whether it's for air miles, renting property, or to have an alarm system installed, you will need a credit check before you can be approved.

Here is a personal example of how uncommon some requests to check your credit are. I went to a seminar about online marketing, and they were selling web site packages that promised to make you millions. That's not a direct quote of course, but that's how the message came across. When it was over, I started filling out a form that told them what I liked most about their seminar. They also wanted to know how to contact me in the future. Well, I began writing down my comments, and then stopped to read the fine print at the bottom of the page. In laymen's terms, it stated that credit checks may be done on the person filling out the form. I had seen this claim on contracts before, but I was surprised to read it on a customer survey. I guess they were offering financing for their products, but obviously, only wanted to work with those people who had built a good credit history. I made a point of going up to one of the sales reps to tell him that I would not be signing the paper. When he asked why, I explained that by so doing, I would be giving his company legal permission to look at my credit whenever they wanted to. He responded, "We hardly ever do that." It was irrelevant whether they did or didn't check my credit; the point was that they could whenever they wanted. Before I left, I saw many of the other attendees sign their papers and hand them in. I wanted to shout out, "People, what are we doing? READ THE FINE PRINT!"

In the mortgage world, mortgage professionals are audited, or reviewed, by credit-reporting agencies every once in a while to ensure that we were given your written permission before checking your credit. Be cautious, though, as some companies don't ask for any type of confirmation from you before looking at your credit. Also, be aware that when you are dealing with companies that you have already worked with, most client contracts include a clause that allows lenders to check your credit without additional written consent. The only way you can guarantee that a company won't look at your credit without your consent is by not giving them your personal information to begin with.

The good news is that inquiries will eventually come off of your credit report. However, both TransUnion and Equifax state a different time frame for this to happen on their web sites. TransUnion says that *"Each hard inquiry will be displayed on your credit profile for a minimum of six years, but may remain longer."* (www.transunion.ca) Equifax doesn't put as much emphasis on a full six years for inquiries. They say, *"The following inquiries were generated because the listed company has requested a copy of your credit report. An inquiry, made by a Creditor, will automatically purge three years from the date it is made. The system will keep record of a minimum of 5 inquiries."* (www.equifax.ca) This means that you may see inquiries prior to the three-year date on your report, but that is only if you don't have five recent inquiries made within the last three years.

The average Joe isn't the only one who doesn't know how an inquiry can affect your credit. Unfortunately, neither do the majority of sales reps calling you from companies, large or small. That means it is completely up to you to protect your personal information. Only you can prevent the lowering of your score by having too many credit checks done.

Rule 7 – Average Joe Action Steps

1. Next time you apply for credit, print off a copy of your credit report and use that to shop for the best interest rates.

2. Read the fine print on any application, as you could be giving someone permission to check your credit now and in the future.

Chapter 11

Rule 8: Closing Your Credit Account(s) Lowers Your Score

Ever cut up your credit cards or close your credit accounts? Closing any type of credit account can drop your score dramatically. This is an area where people, who think they know the rules of credit, get hurt the most often. I find that the average Joe understands that he must pay his bills on time, but he doesn't realize that cancelling his credit accounts will affect his credit negatively.

It won't matter what the reason is, because the predetermined computer code which the credit-reporting agencies use, shows a cancelled credit account as a negative. Many argue that this rule doesn't make any sense. Unfortunately, credit-reporting agencies don't take into consideration that you're trying to protect yourself by cancelling your credit.

When I first started in the industry, I found out the hard way exactly how important this rule is and how much it can lower your score. I met Rob and Elise when they were looking to purchase a new property. When he and his wife sat down with me, and we went over the numbers, everything looked good, so I requested their credit reports, and both their scores were fine. We submitted the application to the bank for the purchase and everything was approved and ready to go.

A problem arose, however, as they applied for a home equity line of credit for their existing home, through their bank. They acquired this financing in order to have a larger down payment for their new property. Everything went smoothly except when it came closer to the final weeks before they were to move. About five months after I had originally reviewed their credit, the bank with which I had the mortgage approved on the new house, asked me to get an updated credit report for them. When I looked at Rob's new credit score, it had dropped 50 points lower than the first time I checked.

I wondered what he had done wrong, so I compared his first credit report to the new one. Everything seemed to be exactly the same. No missed payments, no increase of funds, and no new credit. The only difference was that a credit card and a personal line of credit had been closed. What I didn't know was that part of the condition for them to get the home equity line of credit with his current bank required him to close two credit accounts he had with competing banks. Rob had no clue this would hurt his credit. Although he'd had those credit accounts for a while, he didn't use them much anymore, because he had newer credit cards that offered him rewards and a lower interest rate. However, Rob and Elise's ability to qualify for the type of mortgage product and rate they were looking for on the purchase had been based on them being in a certain category with their credit scores. Now, because of this huge drop in Rob's score, they no longer qualified. After a lot of explaining, producing of documentation, and even a little bit of begging, an exception was made. The saving grace was that these accounts, which their bank made them cancel, weren't joint accounts. They were only in Rob's name, leaving Elise's score the same.

It is quite common for banks and mortgage companies to request that you pay off debt so that you can qualify, but asking you to close accounts with competitor's is another thing all together. Paying down balances will help your credit, but closing them will only lower your score. I haven't heard of branch mortgage specialists doing this for a long time, but it is something to keep an eye open for. If you notice that this is one of the conditions of your mortgage, talk to your mortgage rep about working around it. If the bank tells you that there is no way around it, you can always go apply to another bank. At the very least, you will be aware that if you close credit accounts your score is going to drop, and it will take some time for it to come back up.

As bad as closing your credit accounts are for your credit score, it is even worse if the financial institution has to do it for you! This only happens when there is a problem with your account, which is generally caused by several missed payments. The most common reasons people find themselves in this situation is because they either thought they had already paid off the balance, or they felt they weren't responsible for the outstanding amount in the first place. No matter what the situation is, closing or cancelling credit cards or lines of credit will affect your credit negatively. Remember that a bad credit history will not be erased just because you closed the offending account. This can still be viewed for many years after you have closed the account.

Be aware of "upgrading" your credit accounts

Even if you are "upgrading" your card, you may be hurting your credit. I made this mistake with my longest-running credit card. When I just started in the industry, unaware of this rule, I upgraded my basic Visa credit card to a Gold status, which offered rewards. What I didn't know was that the bank had my old card listed as "closed by consumer" on my credit report, and that the Gold Visa was now starting out as a brand new account. Banks don't do this to purposefully hurt our credit; they do it to keep their system organized. Although my wife and I had a great vacation paid partially with my reward points, my repayment history with my longest-running credit card was now gone. That is over 85 months, just over seven years, of credit history wasted in one phone call. Knowing what I know now, I would have told the bank that I wanted to keep the old card and to sign me up for a new one too. That way I could have used the old card once every six months just to keep it active, and the new card for the majority of my spending. This warning applies to loans as well, which happens most commonly with vehicle financing. If you switch your financing from one vehicle to another or even increase the loan amount on your existing account, the bank will close that account and start a new one. This has the same affect that closing any type of account does.

Another growing trend happening today is that people are closing their credit accounts in fear of identity theft. It is true that inactive credit accounts are targets for fraudsters. However, this can be controlled by actively checking your balances, instead of actually closing your accounts. Just stop using your account or cut up your credit cards, and after one or two years, your account(s) will be deactivated. Remember letting your accounts go inactive won't hurt you, but it doesn't help your credit either. If you have to close an account, I advise you not to do so if you're going to apply for credit in the near future. This will give your score time to rebound, before you apply for any new credit. As stated in Rule 3, when closing any credit account, make sure you still have at least two established accounts. By signing up for a new card with a point or reward system, you may get that dream trip faster, but you may also be losing your credit status at the same time.

It also matters which cards you choose to cancel or allow to go inactive. The longer you have had the credit account established, the more it will hurt your credit when you cancel it. When reviewing your credit, you can see the status or condition of each account.

Equifax Example

Car Loan Ltd.

Phone Number:	(905) 321-1119	High Credit/Credit Limit	0000006936
Account Number:	XXX....285	Payment Amount:	$144.00
Association in Account:	Joint	Balance:	$7,161.00
Type of Account:	Installment	Past Due:	$2,312.00
Date Opened:	2007-02	Date of Last Activity:	2009-10
Status:	**Closed by Consumer**		
		Date Reported:	2010-10
Months Reviewed:	No payment 30 days late		
Payment History:	No payment 60 days late		
	No payment 90 days late		

TransUnion Example

Your Bank

Account #:	****123	**Type:**	Type: Revolving Account	**Opened:**	08/17/2005
Condition:	(Open)	**Pay:**	Paid as Agreed	**Reported:**	02/04/2012
Balance:	....	**Status:**	Satus: Open	**Responsibility:**	Individual
High Balance:	$10,000	**Payment:**	$0 Monthly (due every		Account
Terms			month)	**Past Due:**	
		Limit:			

Remarks: Line of Credit

Amt In High Credit Column (Disp 122–130 of Trade Segment) is Credit Limit

Two Year Payment History:

TransUnion	OK	OK	OK	OK	OK	OK	OK	OK	OK	OK	OK	OK	OK	OK	OK	OK	OK	OK	OK	OK	OK	OK	OK	OK
	feb	mar	apr	my	jun	jul	aug	sep	oct	nov	dec	11	feb	mar	apr	my	jun	jul	aug	sep	oct	nov	dec	12

Six Year Payment History:

30 Days Late: 0   60 Days Late: 0   90 Days Late: 0

Although the age of the applicant is irrelevant to your credit report, it makes sense that the longer you can prove a clean active payment history, the less risky you become to the banks. Ending or upgrading any credit account will effectively stop the clock on how long your credit has been established.

Rule 8 – Average Joe Action Steps

1. Review your credit reports to see which accounts have been established the longest and avoid cancelling or upgrading them.

Chapter 12

Rule 9: Don't Let Someone Else Wreck Your Credit

As I've mentioned before, it can take years to build your credit, but it doesn't take long to destroy it. Sometimes it isn't even a lack of knowledge or poor money management that can wreck your credit score, forcing you to start all over. It is becoming more common for someone else to hurt your credit for you. That is why the last, and very important rule, is to protect your credit.

Protect your personal information

Don't throw away your statements. Buy a good paper shredder so that no one can recycle your personal information. This advice is not just for businesses, but also for the average Joe. When I first started in the mortgage industry, I knew that legally I had to dispose of sensitive information by shredding it. It wasn't until after learning about credit that I started to use the shredder for my own personal documents too. To better understand the importance of this, take a look at some of your financial statements, and then try to imagine what a criminal could do with them. Your name, address(es), phone number(s) and even your account number(s) could be used by a fraudster to take advantage of you. Can you imagine how much damage could be done? If your wallet is stolen, you usually notice right away, and can have your accounts cancelled quickly. Most financial statements come out once a month or on a quarterly basis. Just imagine how much harm a criminal could do over a period of one month. Scary? Yes, but sometimes that's what it takes for us to get our act together.

There are many ways and programs to protect yourself online, but the best method is to review your financial statements regularly. This is something I'm a little lazy about myself, but fortunately for me, my wife is much more diligent. Regular review will not only protect you against fraud, but from human or computer error as well. I often see mistakes on people's credit reports, and generally, by the time I let them know about them, extensive delays have prevented them from being approved for financing quickly.

Your personal information needs to be protected not only in paper form, but in all aspects. Be careful what information you confirm over the phone. If someone calls you and asks you for your personal information, don't give it to them, even if it's a reputable company. If they are calling to verify your information with simple yes and no questions, then it's probably not a big deal. What you should do if you're in doubt is hang up and dial the number on the back of your bank client card or credit card to verify their information first. This way you know for sure who you're talking to. If you have to speak to a specific agent, get their full name before you hang up. Then, when you call back, you can ask for that person directly.

Money-saving tip

The Canadian Council of Better Business Bureaus has estimated that identity theft may cost Canadian consumers, banks and credit card firms, stores and other businesses more than $2 billion annually. No matter whether you have fraud insurance or protection on your credit accounts or not, it is still a cost that eventually gets passed along to us, the average Joe consumer. So you want to save money? Then protect your credit and information, as this is one of the fastest growing crimes in Canada. (source http://www.justice.gc.ca/eng/news-nouv/nr-cp/2007/doc_32179.html)

Your Social Insurance Number (SIN) is the key

This number is very important, as it easily identifies you. It is the only piece of identification that won't be the same as anyone else's. It is a no-brainer that you should keep your SIN from being lost or stolen. Although it's important to keep your number safe, remember that on almost all credit applications nothing can be submitted or finalized without your SIN. That is why it is so important to find out who you are working with before you pass on any information. It always surprises me how liberal people are with their personal information. The majority of my mortgage business comes to me online. I have clients all across Canada. I rarely meet even the customers who reside in my own city. In fact, I have never met 95% of my clients. For anyone who has applied for a mortgage before, you will know how much personal information the banks require for mortgage financing. I have had more than a few clients, after gathering all the information necessary to process a mortgage application, joke that I now knew more about them than they did.

Although the police and governing bodies are constantly trying to catch fraudsters, here are some basic ways to protect yourself:

• Find out who you are dealing with before you send any information.

• Take the sales rep information and the business information and verify it.

• You can contact the Better Business Bureau (BBB) to see if the information you have received matches with their information.

• Check government web sites and association web sites to verify their information:
www.antifraudcentre.ca
www.rcmp-grc.gc.ca/scams-fraudes/index-eng.htm

• Type "fraudulent companies in Canada" into a search engine and you will find numerous web sites designed to report and warn Canadians about popular scams.

Please note that all of the links to these web sites can also be found on: www.TheAverageJoeBook.com

If you are dealing with professionals within a certain industry, you can verify their information based with their governing body. Governing bodies are organizations, which exist solely to bring and maintain a certain level of standard of whatever professional category they are in. Some have web sites that are designed specifically for the general public. For example, for mortgages, almost every province has a governing body that each person in that field has to be registered with. You can easily check on an agent's status or make a complaint on these sites. Generally, it's as easy as putting in the person's last name to view their status and contact information. By no means is this a complete list, but even by being a bit more aware, it will help you keep your credit safe.

Get everything in writing

I have a big tip for you: Don't EVER take someone's word for it; get it in writing. It is very common to have bills or collections continue reporting as unpaid even though they have been paid off. The problem is that you can't prove that you have paid off a debt if you don't have something in writing. When working with banks, it means nothing unless you get written proof. The other key point to keep in mind is once you get written confirmation, store it somewhere that you can remember. Having documentation will also reduce the amount of time it takes to have the credit-reporting agencies remove the error from your reports.

One of my clients, Dave, had a collection of approximately $8 on his credit report. Every six months or so, he would get a bill from a cell phone company for an account that had been closed a year earlier. He just kept paying it, because he couldn't quite remember if he had paid the bill before, and he thought a bill of less than $10 wasn't worth fighting over. Each time he paid it, the clerk assured him that the account was now paid in full. Dave's problem was that he didn't get confirmation in writing. The bills stopped coming only once he demanded to receive written confirmation of his bill payment. In a case like Dave's, don't pay unless the charging company can give you something in writing, right then, stating that the account has a zero balance. After a couple of months, you would be wise to verify that it has been taken off of your credit report. I guarantee you that no one else is going to follow up on your account to make sure everything is recorded properly. That is completely up to you.

Be careful of credit-fixing scams

Credit isn't meant to be repaired within a couple of days. It takes time to re-establish your credit, so be wary of quick-fix programs. Although there are some legitimate programs to help speed up the process of repairing credit, there are some out there that will do more harm than good. While I don't have any personal or client horror stories to tell on this subject, I do know that there are very few laws pertaining to credit counselling, and because of this, you need to be on guard. However, I can promise you that by following the Nine Rules of Credit, you will establish or re-establish your credit much faster than if you don't follow them.

Secured credit better than co-signing

I think that we're all somewhat aware of how dangerous it is for fraudsters to get a hold of our credit, but what about the possibility of our loved ones unwittingly wreaking havoc with it? If you're trying to help a spouse, a child, or some other relative establish credit, I would recommend that you get them started with a secured card instead of co-signing for them.

A secured credit card, unlike co-signing, can limit your risk because the only loss to you would be whatever amount you put on deposit for another person. When co-signing, you are attaching your name to someone else's account, so if a payment isn't made, it will affect both person's credit. Co-signing won't automatically hurt your credit, but just like joint credit, you will be held 100% responsible for the activities on that account, no matter who is at fault. As important as establishing credit is, keep in mind that for some people, especially the inexperienced, credit can be a recipe for disaster. The risks and extra costs of co-signing can be learned from the following experience I had with a client of mine.

Eric was applying for a mortgage, and he was self-employed. For those of you who are self-employed, the major banks want to see an even better credit score than from those who are employees. In this case, Eric was just under the minimum required credit score to qualify through a major bank. When I asked him about the one credit card that showed a very poor credit repayment history, he told me that it was a card he had co-signed for his nephew. Due to this card and the very tight qualifying restrictions he was under, he had to get his mortgage from a smaller lender who charged him a 1.35% higher interest rate and a 4% additional fee. This may not seem like a lot, but over five years, it cost him an extra $54,733.19 on his mortgage. Sometimes, the banks will make exceptions when there is a good explanation, but in this case, because of other exceptions needing to be made on his file, the major banks wouldn't approve him. I advised him that he should pay out the balance on that joint card and close it. Although this would have fixed his credit and saved him money in the long term, he didn't want to do it. He didn't like the fact that he would be giving his nephew a way out of his responsibilities. I have to commend Eric for his resolve on the principle he was trying to instill in his nephew. However, in the meantime, his credit will continue to suffer until either his nephew learns to manage his credit or until the account is closed down.

When ordering your credit reports

For your own protection, I suggest that you don't order credit reports from web sites that claim to give you access to both credit reports for one low price. Some may be legitimate, but many are not. Think it through; go to the source or follow a link to the source so you know that it is the right site. You will be entering in a lot of personal information. What's the point of saving a few bucks, if you put yourself at risk of credit fraud?

Fraud watch programs

Both credit-reporting agencies are very active in advertising their fraud watch programs. Are they necessary? No! Can they be beneficial? You bet! I believe that for those of you who are rebuilding your credit or who are a bit lazy when it comes to reviewing your statements, these programs are great. Basically, each of these fraud watch programs give you access to your individual credit reports, notify you of any irregular activity, and give you 24/7 access to an agent to help you understand what is happening on your account. Each of these programs cost you about $15.00 a month. If you are interested in finding out more on what is offered by each credit reporting agency please visit www.transunion.ca and www.equifax.ca for more details.

No matter if you sign up for one of these programs or not, it is very important to protect and review your credit constantly. I would suggest that you view your credit report at least once a year with each reporting agency. This will insure that you can correct errors quickly and always maintain amazing credit.

The end to the Nine Rules of Credit

So that's it; the Nine Rules of Credit that the average Joe needs to know in order to start, rebuild, and maintain excellent credit. Not to worry though, it isn't the end of this book. Please keep in mind that, although I call these the Nine Rules of Credit, sometimes it's necessary to ignore a few of them in order to achieve something bigger. For example, opening multiply credit accounts will lower your credit score. However, if you don't have credit, then opening a few accounts are necessary. Don't get me wrong; every time you break a rule, it brings negative consequences. However, being aware of these rules puts you in control by letting you weigh the advantages, as well as the risks, before making your decision. You can also limit mistakes and speed up your recovery time now that you understand what the credit-reporting agencies grade you on. It's kind of like writing an open-book test, and having a cheat sheet. Don't worry, though, this isn't being dishonest. It's just playing to win!

Rule 9 – Avergae Joe Action Steps

1. Devise a plan to review your credit and accounts regularly.

2. Review the Nine Rules of Credit on a regular basis, so you don't forget them.

Chapter 13

The Big Picture

The quote, "The only thing constant in life is change" applies to your credit score, as well as life. Each month, any action or inaction will change your credit score. I've included this chapter to help recap the Nine Rules of Credit, but also to illustrate how one transaction can affect your credit both positively and negatively at the same time. On the next page you will see a visual example of how each of the Nine Rules of Credit are weighed to make up your final credit score.

The power that comes from not only knowing the rules, but how important each one is, will put you in the driver seat and allow you to make the best decisions possible regarding your credit.

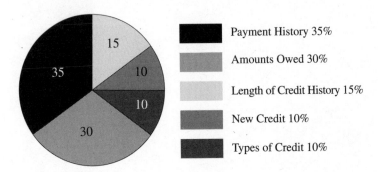

Please keep in mind that this graph is a generic display of the main categories and a basic review of the Nine Rules of Credit. Equifax and TransUnion are competitors, so they will not openly reveal the exact algorithm they each use. The algorithm or electronic code that each reporting agency uses is also constantly upgraded to better reflect credit risk for the lending institutions.

Using the Credit Categories pie graph illustrated above, I will demonstrate how the basic action of applying for a loan can affect your credit. I will also refer back to my earlier story about the Swagger Wagon my wife bought. To understand the effects of this new loan on my wife's credit, you will need to know how her credit looked both before and after she applied. Previous to applying, Jess requested a copy of both her credit reports so she could, confidently, shop around for the best interest rates without having her credit checked each time. The numbers and results below are based on the information taken from her Equifax Report. Her TransUnion Report reflected a similar scenario, except the score was a bit higher due to small differences between the two agencies.

The main categories were ranked alike by both reporting agencies, with just a few minor differences.

Before

Before this loan application, Jess had three credit accounts, which included two different credit cards and a line of credit. Here are a couple of Credit Report-Card Charts that I will use to help me visually explain the before and after effects of Jess's loan. The categories found in the Credit Report-Card Charts are the same ones found in the previously shown Credit Categories pie graph, only with further explanations written below them. I have also added a column named "Mark," so you can see how she was doing with each rule or category. This mark is based on a scale of one to ten, ten being the best.

Credit Report Card: Jess's Credit *Before* the Loan

	Credit Category	Rule	% Weighted	Mark
A.	Payment History	1, 5, 9	35%	10
B.	Amounts Owed	2, 9	30%	10
C.	Length of Credit	3, 6, 8, 9	15%	9
D.	New Credit	7, 9	10%	10
E.	Types of Credit	4, 9	10%	7
Credit Score		**799**		

Reasons for each mark are explained as follows:

Payment history category

Jess had never been late or missed a payment on any of her accounts. Although she used her accounts often, one of them hadn't been used during the past six months. Because two out of three accounts were active and she had a perfect payment history, she received a mark of ten out of ten. If she would have had a late payment within the last 12 months, it would have lowered her score by about 40 to 50 points. Multiple late payments, or even missed payments, would have really lowered her score. Missing her payments all together would have led to a collection company registering a collection on her credit report, which would have lowered her score upward of 100 points.

Amounts owed category

Her balances had never been more than 50% of her credit limits. This may well be due to the fact that whenever she made large purchases, they always seemed to magically appear on my accounts, rather than on hers! In this category, if the balance of one of her accounts had been closer to her limits, it would have dropped her score by 20 to 30 points. If her balance ever went over her limit, you could expect her score to drop at least 30 to 40 points.

Length of credit history category

The average time that her credit accounts had been open was 52 months (four years and four months); her newest account being established for just over three years. All limits were $2,500 or higher. Had each account been active for at least five years, this would have put her mark at ten out of ten, rather than eight out of ten. Although having a credit limit of $2,500 or more doesn't matter to your credit score, as you learned in Rule 3, a credit card limit of $500 doesn't look very established to a mortgage lender, when providing financing for a mortgage of $300,000, for example.

New credit category

Jess had five inquiries made over the last seven years. When a lending institution looks at your credit, one or less hard inquiry (credit inquiries made by lenders that lower your score) each year is considered really good.

Types of credit category

As previously mentioned, Jess had three accounts, all of them revolving, and one of them being a line of credit. She had no loans or open type accounts like a diners card or a cell phone account. Since she only had revolving accounts (credit cards or lines of credit), it dropped her mark for this section to six out of ten. Luckily for Jess, this account only weighs in up to a max of 10% of your credit score. This is why she still had such a high credit score.

Based on the Nine Rules of Credit, Jess was doing an awesome job of keeping her score high. The only three ways she could have improved her points would have been by using her one inactive account at least every four to six months, and by having all of her accounts established longer than five years. Having different types of credit, such as a loan, would have increased her mark in this category, but there would also be some possible disadvantages. I discuss these further along in this chapter. Having done well with the majority of the rules, Jess's credit score was just under 800, which is considered "Amazing." She makes me so proud!

After

Now, here is what happened once she applied and was approved for the new "Swagger Wagon" loan.

Credit Report card: Jess's Credit *After* the Loan

	Credit Category	Rule	% Weighted	Up	Down	N/A	New Mark	Old Mark
A	Payment History	1, 5, 9	35%			X	10	10
B	Amounts Owed	2, 9	30%		X		8	10
C	Length of Credit	3, 6, 8, 9	15%		X		7	9
D	New Credit	7, 9	10%		X		9	10
E	Types of Credit	4, 9	10%	X			10	7
Credit Score			752					

Reasons for each mark are explained as follows:

Payment history category

No change would have occurred in this area as there weren't any missed payments and the new loan for the minivan is considered active.

Amounts owed category

Remember, Equifax and TransUnion don't necessarily care how much someone owes; they are more concerned about the ratio of your balance compared to that of your limit. They feel that this is a better indicator of whether you are a credit risk or not. According to what we discussed in Rule 2, you already know that you need to keep your balance amounts 50% or lower on each of your account limits. Let's say that Jess, in the above scenario, was approved for a loan amount of $15,000. That means, as of day one, she would still owe $15,000. Remember, the price of the car or the amount of your down payment is irrelevant when considering your credit. Therefore, her credit limit and balance will stay the same, until she makes her first payment. Because her balance is 100% of what she borrowed on the original loan, her credit will be negatively affected until she has paid off at least half of it. Although loans can be taken out for different lengths of time, in this example, the loan is for a period of five years. This means that the loan will lower her credit score for just over two-and-a-half years. It is in this category, Amounts Owed, that her score will be hurt the most because it is weighted so heavily!

How do you get around obtaining a car loan and not having it hurt your credit? You can look at using a line of credit, as long as long as your limit is high enough to accommodate the balance needed. The other option is to get approved for the highest loan amount possible, by putting the lowest down payment upfront. After you have the loan, apply as much money available to lower the balance. Since your credit score is a summary of all your accounts, if you need to apply for financing that may lower your score, the better established your other accounts are, the less it will bring your score down.

Length of credit history category

Jess's score would also be lowered in this category due to the fact that she opened a new account. As mentioned before, the credit-reporting agencies want to see your accounts established for as long as possible, but state that the ideal amount of time would be more than four years. I noted earlier that Jess had two of her accounts longer than four years. However, she also had a newer account for just over three years. This made the average time of her accounts being opened only four years and three months. Because she now had a new car loan, it lowered the average time her credit has been established. It took her established credit down from that ideal four-year mark to an average of three years and two months. Since Length of credit is the second biggest category, weighted at 15%, it can put a huge dent in your total score.

New credit category

New credit, although important, only makes up 10% of ones total score, as explained more thoroughly in Rule 7. Jess's score would be lowered anywhere between five and ten points, by having one hard inquiry made (which is when a lending institution checks your credit). Based on the fact that she has had very few inquiries done in the past, I would estimate that this one inquiry only lowered her score by five points.

Types of credit category

The one positive increase to her score was found in the category, Types of Credit. Unfortunately for Jess, this category only makes up a maximum of 10% of her credit score. However, this new loan will increase her credit score because both TransUnion and Equifax see obtaining and managing a selection of different types of credit as a sign of credit strength. As long as Jess maintains this new loan as well as she has her other accounts, it will show that she is responsible enough to manage this new installment, loan payment as well as her revolving trade lines, her credit cards and line of credit.

Isn't this crazy! This is why I am so passionate about credit. There is nothing common about how the credit-reporting agencies rank your everyday actions in regards to being credit worthy. If knowing about credit and how it can affect you isn't common sense, and you obviously don't learn about it in school, then how does the average Joe learn about credit? The answer is this. You either go through life completely unaware or you learn the hard way, through personal experience.

I hope I have instilled, in each readers mind that credit is a tool. Credit, like money, is designed to be used, but just as Sir Isaac Newton stated, "To every action there is always an equal and opposite reaction." There is nothing wrong with applying for a loan or any other type of credit, but there is a reaction for every action or inaction with credit. My goal is to protect you from making any unconscious mistakes. My wife's score, even after dropping from 799 to 752, was OK because she received a great interest rate, got the van she wanted, and still is in the "Amazing" credit category. However, this story wouldn't have been of the "Happily Ever After" variety if Jess's credit hadn't been so strong. It doesn't take much to drop your score and put you in a category that could cost you more, or even keep you from being approved. Also, keep in mind that I reviewed her credit right after the new loan showed up, so with each month that she puts between her and the new credit account, her score will improve.

Chapter 14

Some Important Things to Remember

Your credit score is only one determining factor when it comes to judging your eligibility for financing. Other contributing factors are known as the Five Cs of Credit. Please visit my web site www.TheAverageJoeBook.com for a blog post that goes into more details about the Five Cs of Credit. For this book, it is suffice to say each bank and lending institution use many different criteria when approving you for a loan. However, banks consider your credit as one of the most important factors for qualifying you.

My warning about secured credit cards

Keep in mind that secured credit acts exactly like a regular credit account, so all of the Nine Rules of Credit will still apply. Actually,

I would argue, it is even more imperative to follow all the rules when starting out, due to the fact that there is not as much established credit history to offset any mistakes. When the average Joe gets a secured credit card, the most common errors he makes are found in the following rules:

- Rule 2 – High Balances Equal low Score
- Rule 8 – Closing Your Credit Account(s) Lowers Your Score

Keeping a balance below 50% becomes increasingly difficult the lower the limit. As most secured cards start off with such a low limit, it's even more important that you watch the amount you are spending.

People seem to have the most trouble with Rule 8. Generally, the moment someone is approved for an unsecured credit card, they cancel their secured card so they can get their deposit back. The problem with this is that when you close the secured card, it no longer builds your credit. In fact, closing an account lowers your score, as we've seen in Chapter 11. Therefore, you should keep your secured card open, and use it occasionally, even after you've been approved for traditional credit. Once you have established two or more additional credit accounts for at least two years, then you can cancel the secured card if you really need your deposit back. If you do cancel your secured credit card though, make sure that you don't do it right before you apply for new financing.

Disputing errors

Small mistakes, such as a wrong home address or if where you're currently working hasn't been updated, can be corrected directly through the reporting agencies. When you review your credit and you notice an error on an individual account, you need to contact the lender and the credit-reporting agencies right away. Any supporting documentation that you have will be very helpful, and you should expect it to be required. Even if you don't have the documentation handy, it is still worth a try to correct any errors on your reports. It will just take longer to get things fixed. If Equifax or TransUnion have done an investigation, and there is still not enough evidence in your favour, then you can always have a note added to your file. You can also add a note even if you know it was your error due to extenuating circumstances that you think future creditors should know about. For example, you are aware that you missed a payment on your credit card. However, this was because you just started a new job and the payroll department didn't have your correct banking information and, therefore, couldn't deposit your paycheque. Both credit-reporting agencies have guidelines that must be followed in order to post a comment on your credit report.

TransUnion states this on their web site:

"If our investigation does not resolve the dispute, you may add a 100-word consumer statement to your report. Exception: 200 words in Saskatchewan. Statements should be relevant to the credit information in dispute. Please note that TransUnion will not accept statements that are defamatory or otherwise illegal or inappropriate. Requests for statements to be added or removed should be placed in writing with your signature on them."

Equifax states this about credit disputes:

"In either case, you may add a statement to our file explaining any concerns you have. Equifax will include your statement on all future credit reports, if it contains 400 words or less."

Although Equifax doesn't include this warning in their notes, they will also disregard any comments that are graphic or contentious in nature. Try to keep all emotion out of your statement.

To get the mailing addresses, submission guidelines, and templates please visit the individual web sites of each credit reporting agency or on my web site www.TheAverageJoeBook.com.

I think that the feature of allowing consumers to add written notes to their own credit report(s) is overlooked by many people. For mortgage financing, we use explanations and notes to mitigate around possible perceived weaknesses, in order to get applications approved. With other types of financing, you may not have a representative that will tell you what is on your credit report. If a bank finds something they don't like on your application, they may ask for more details, but most of the time, they won't. They rarely give you any details, except whether or not you have been approved. Having a simple note on your credit report could make the difference between you qualifying for financing or not. You may even be bumped into a better credit category and receive a lower interest rate and lower fees.

Tyler, one of my clients, had some bruises on his credit, but after explaining that these missed payments were due to him being in a severe car accident, the lender gave him the required financing. Having notes on your credit file will help underwriters understand your circumstances, and they will take that information into consideration. You may even get lucky enough to deal with someone who has gone through the same situation as you, and therefore, advocates for your approval or a lower rate because of it.

Having mistakes corrected can be time-consuming and difficult. The most frustrating part is that you'll usually be under a time crunch trying to get a loan when you discover the discrepancy, and now, it will take time for the credit-reporting agencies to correct the mistake.

Mistakes found on a credit report are very common; I have heard the numbers being even as high as 80% of credit reports having some errors on them. Of course, it doesn't matter about everyone else; it only matters that yours doesn't have any mistakes.

Here is a personal example of how these mistakes can happen to anybody.

One day, I received a call from a collection agency about my Visa card. They informed me that it was going to be registered for collections. I was shocked by this news, and I obviously wanted it sorted out right away. After confirming my address, my social insurance number, and some of my other personal information, the woman apologized for the inconvenience and told me that there must be another Richard Moxley.

Both credit-reporting agencies state it will take about 30-days to conclude an investigation; however, sometimes it may take even longer. It takes time to get all of the necessary documentation together, in addition to having mistakes removed, which could delay your application by months or even years. Everything depends on what you are trying to have corrected. That is why I advise you to check your credit report regularly and correct any mistakes as soon as possible.

Chapter 14 – Average Joe Action Steps

1. If you find that you have any missed payments, and it was due to circumstances beyond your control, add a note to your credit file with both TransUnion and Equifax.

Chapter 15

My Mission

Now that you have read the instruction manual, it is time for you to put everything into practice. If you haven't noticed yet, I am extremely passionate about credit. You may still have some questions about the subject, but I didn't write this book with the intent of making you all experts. My hope is to get you to understand the importance of credit, to learn the Nine Rules of Credit, and to motivate you to continue to monitor your credit. If you haven't requested copies of both your credit reports, now is the time to do so.

I would consider it a great compliment if I knew you finished reading this book because of my great writing skills and my wonderful sense of humour. However, since that is probably not the case, I truly hope you take the book's message away with you. Like you,

I have noticed that there is a great lack of knowledge and understanding when it comes to credit. How would anyone know about the rules required to be involved in the credit game? We don't learn these rules in school, nor does someone sit you down and give you the credit talk when you turn 18! In fact, I'd bet some parents would rather give their kids the birds and the bees talk instead of the credit speech. There are tons of books, web site blogs, and TV segments that offer you little tidbits of information from here or there, but everyone seems to be giving different advice. I hope you see the value of this book in understanding how each of the Nine Rules of Credit affect your credit score and how best to quickly repair and maintain that score throughout your lifetime.

If you thought the content was useful, then please PASS IT ON! My mission is to get this book, with its Nine Rules of Credit, out to 30,000 Canadians before November 27, 2015.

Money-saving tip

If you are a teacher, a professor, or are looking to order the book in larger quantities, please email me directly at Richard@TheAverageJoeBook.com to see how you can get a free copy or great discounts!

To help you with passing the message on, here are some of the things that you will find on my web site www.TheAverageJoeBook.com.

Tools and lists

• Canadian Financial Calculators – including calculators to help you with mortgages and loan payments, comparing prepayment options, debt snowballing, and more.

• Links – to other good financing web sites that focus on the financial education of Canadians.

• Book list – this is a list of other good books that deal with different financial subjects.

• and much more!

My Blog

As things change with credit and I learn more tips and tricks to help the average Joe, I will be putting these updates on my blog. If you have any comments or tips please feel free to comment on each blog post.

Readers' comments

Your comments are very helpful. Not only do they let me know how the Nine Credit Rules were most helpful to you, they also help those who haven't read the book to know a bit more about how the book can help them. If you are on my web site, please take a moment to add a comment

Spread the word

This part of my web site is specifically designed to make it as easy as possible to spread the word. Of course, you can always buy or lend a copy of my book to your friends, but there are lots of other ways you can help. This section is loaded with social media links, templates, and other referral ideas.

Affiliates

What the Average Joe Needs to Know wants to connect you with other companies that have a passion for financial education and great products. Be sure to check them out and by going through my web site you always receive the best pricing!

Whether or not you decide to help me in my mission to inform Canadian consumers about the risks and benefits of credit, I hope that at least you have learned something new. If you have any questions, feel free to email me at Richard@TheAverageJoeBook.com.

Thank you for reading my book and good luck to you in all your financial endeavours! From one average Joe to another, I genuinely care!

ABOUT THE AUTHOR

Richard Moxley AMP, and CEO of Average Joe Education has a passion for educating Canadians about finances. Growing up in an average middle class home didn't stop him from having a very active mind and interest when it came to money. While others were playing tag on the elementary school play ground, Richard was selling marbles back to the kids he just won them from. His entrepreneurial mindset, over six years of being a licensed mortgage agent, and personal experience in many other financial fields is what makes this book truly unique. To learn more visit his web site at www.TheAverageJoeBook.com